OPTIMIZING
TRANSACT-SQL:

Advanced Programming Techniques

David Rozenshtein, Ph.D.

Anatoly Abramovich, Ph.D.

Eugene Birger, Ph.D.

SQL FORUM PRESS

Publisher of SQL Forum Journal

40087 Mission Boulevard, Suite 167, Fremont, CA 94539
(800) 943-9300 Voice ▪ (510) 656-5116 Fax

Library of Congress Catalog Card Number 95-72657

ISBN 0-9649812-0-3

© 1995 SQL Forum Press

Cover Design: Tom McKeith

Editor: Tom Bondur

Publisher of SQL Forum Journal

40087 Mission Boulevard, Suite 167, Fremont, CA 94539
(800) 943-9300 Voice ▪ (510) 656-5116 Fax

Contents

Foreword

I hear whispers– "Hey! Have you tried characteristic functions yet?" I hear enthusiastic shouts– "Wow! I found a new way to use characteristic functions today!" All because *I have 'discovered' characteristic functions!*

About three years ago, I encountered an article by David Rozenshtein, Anatoly Abramovich, and Eugene Birger in *SQL Forum Journal* that introduced me to the use of characteristic functions in SQL. At first, I thought characteristic functions were intriguing puzzles. Over time, I realized that this was an important, new method for SQL programming that could greatly improve the performance of queries I was writing.

Every few months for almost three years, a new article appeared presenting additional techniques for solving processing problems using characteristic functions. Now these articles from *SQL Forum Journal* are collected into one book.

When I first recommended using these techniques, developers were a little taken aback. At first, characteristic functions are a little hard to read– all of those SIGN and ABS functions! But over time, the expressions start looking familiar, and become 'readable.'

Characteristic functions must be taken in small doses. Read a chapter, write a few queries, and then read the next chapter. As you read the chapters, work through the code, use it three times in a sentence (well– in an application.) It will add to your working 'vocabulary' of techniques. This stuff is cool.

Every time I review stored procedures for a developer, I find some way that I can use characteristic functions to improve performance. Characteristic functions improve readability too– though this may be hard to believe at first!

Sometimes you will be able to replace several SQL statements with one (not too simple) statement. With judicious use of comments, people reading your code will understand what you are up to. As with any technique you are going to use to improve performance, make sure you are reviewing the results. Check to make sure that you *really* made the query faster!

Microsoft SQL Server Version 6 includes a CASE expression that is part of SQL-92. These CASE expressions provide a more readable and standard way to take advantage of characteristic functions. The translation of characteristic functions to CASE expressions is included in the last chapter.

There are many introductory books on SQL on the market. This is one of the great books for journeyman SQL developers. It gives you powerful techniques to address problems you will encounter daily, and if you practice, you too will become a convert.

Jim Panttaja
Panttaja Consulting Group, Inc.
Healdsburg, CA

Single Statement SQL Solutions to the Table Pivoting and Folding Problems

David Rozenshtein, Ph.D., Anatoly Abramovich, Ph.D., and Eugene Birger, Ph.D.

reprinted from SQL Forum Journal, Vol.1, No.12, November/December 1992

1 Introduction

Simply stated, table pivoting problem is that of turning— or, pivoting— long, narrow tables into short, wide ones. A simple example illustrating this problem is presented below in Figures 1 and 2. Here, the initial data is presented in table **data(name, month, amount)** with the desired result going into table **result(name, janamt, febamt, ..., decamt).** (Here, and for the remainder of this article, we use attribute underlining to designate relational keys.)

data =

name	month	amount
"Jones"	1	5000
"Jones"	2	4500
...		
"Jones"	12	6000
"Smith"	1	5500
"Smith"	2	6500
...		
"Smith"	12	3500
...		

Figure 1: Initial data to be pivoted.

result =

name	janamt	febamt	...	decamt
"Jones"	5000	4500		6000
"Smith"	5500	6500		3500
...				

Figure 2: Desired result.

The need for such pivoting occurs very frequently in practice, primarily because, while the narrow table representation is better for data manipulation, the wide table form is better for presenting data to report writers and to the end-users.

Assuming for the moment that table **data** contains a non-NULL amount value for every month for every person included, a simple and perhaps the most obvious solution to this problem involves twelve steps: first, an insert to "seed" the **result** table and to populate the **janamt** column, and then eleven updates— one for each remaining month. The code segment corresponding to this solution is shown in Figure 3 below. (For specificity, we show our examples in Sybase's Transact-SQL. However, the arguments and techniques presented in this article are applicable to other SQL dialects as well.)

```
INSERT result
SELECT name,
       janamt = amount,
       febamt = 0,
       ...
       decamt = 0
FROM data
WHERE (month = 1)

UPDATE result
SET febamt = amount
FROM data
WHERE (result.name = data.name)
   AND (month = 2)
       ...

UPDATE result
SET decamt = amount
FROM data
WHERE (result.name = data.name)
   AND (month = 12)
```

Figure 3: *A conventional solution to the pivoting problem.*

While conceptually straightforward, this solution is actually not a good one. First, it is computationally inefficient. The most natural clustering of this table is first by **name**, and only then possibly by **month**. Thus, in the absence of an additional index on **month**, this code would involve twelve sequential scans of the **data** table.

Even if such index were to be created, and the optimizer chose to use it, it would not help matters much. The relative sizes of the individual rows from the **data** table and of the data disk pages are likely to be such that all twelve rows belonging to any given person would either fit completely within a page or be split over at most two pages. This would in turn mean that, under the natural clustering by **name,** every data page would still have to be accessed in each of the above twelve steps.

The second problem with the above solution becomes apparent when one considers the relevant recovery and concurrency control issues. It is reasonable to require that either all or none of the pivoting be done— in other words, we do not want some columns in **result** to be computed, and some not, due to some failure. Thus, one would need to enhance this *multi-statement* segment of code with transaction boundaries and appropriate commit/rollback logic. (As an aside, these transaction boundaries would also insure that if this code is run concurrently with itself, then the concurrent executions would not confuse their own intermediate result rows with each other.)

It is of course possible to implement pivoting with a single SQL statement using a twelve-way join of table **data** with itself, as shown in Figure 4 below. While not requiring any explicit transaction boundaries to implement atomicity— Transact-SQL would take care of this automatically— this statement is of course very inefficient.

It turns out, however, that it is also possible to implement pivoting not just with a single Transact-SQL statement, but more importantly using a *single scan* through table **data,** with another scan through the intermediate table created by the optimizer to compute aggregates, resulting in implementation that is an order of magnitude more efficient.

```
SELECT d1.name,
       janamt = d1.amount,
       febamt = d2.amount,
       ...
       decamt = d12.amount
FROM data d1, data d2, data d3, ..., data d11, data d12
WHERE (d1.name = d2.name)
    AND (d2.name = d3.name)
    ...
    AND (d11.name = d12.name)
    AND (d1.month = 1)
    AND (d2.month = 2)
    ...
    AND (d12.month = 12)
```

Figure 4: A twelve-way join implementation of pivoting.

The secret of this implementation lies in the proper encoding and use of *point characteristic functions*. We have developed a relational implementation methodology, which will be presented in forthcoming articles, for solving a wide variety of problems using these and other characteristic functions. In this article we draw on this methodology in implementing table pivoting. We begin with the simplest case of numeric data, and then progress to the more complex cases of strings and NULL values.

2   Numeric base, numeric presentation attributes

By *base attribute* we mean that attribute which is used in the WHERE clauses of the insert and update statements of the conventional solution— in our example, attribute **month.** By *presentation attribute* we mean that attribute whose values are being pivoted— in our example, attribute **amount.** Our first solution shown in Figure 5 deals with the case of Figure 1, where both of these attributes are numeric and non-NULL.

```
INSERT result
SELECT name,
        janamt = SUM(amount*(1–abs(sign(month–1)))),
        febamt = SUM(amount*(1–abs(sign(month–2)))),
        ...
        decamt = SUM(amount*(1–abs(sign(month–12))))
FROM data
GROUP BY name
```

Figure 5: *A single statement solution to the pivoting problem.*

Note that expression **(1–abs(sign(month–1)))** acts as a point characteristic function for month = 1— specifically, it returns 1 if month is equal to 1 (January) and returns 0 otherwise. (Built-in function **sign()** returns –1, 0 and +1 for negative numbers, zero and positive numbers respectively; built-in function **abs()** returns the absolute value of its argument.) Consequently, only one— January— of the twelve amount values participating in the sum aggregate retains its original value, with the other eleven being reduced to zero. Thus, expression **SUM(amount*(1–abs(sign(month–1))))** in effect simply returns the January amount, precisely as required. Expression **(1–abs(sign(month–2)))** acts in a similar way, implementing a characteristic function for month = 2 (February), etc.

This code works exactly as desired if all name/month combinations are present. Suppose, however, that some particular combination, say for Jones for February is missing. In that case, the sum aggregate corresponding to the **febamt** value for Jones would be comprised of only eleven components, all of which, not belonging to February, would be zeroed out. The February component would simply be missing, and the sum aggregate would return 0 as the result. Returning 0 in such a case of missing data, however, is intuitively inappropriate; a better approach would be to return NULL. We will return to this issue later in the article.

3 String base, numeric presentation attributes

We now consider a case where the base attribute is of string type, while the presentation attribute is still numeric. In our example, this means representing months as character strings, say of length 3: "Jan", "Feb", ..., "Dec". The pivoting code corresponding to this case is presented below in Figure 6.

```
INSERT result
SELECT name,
       janamt = SUM(amount*charindex(month,"Jan")),
       febamt = SUM(amount*charindex(month,"Feb")),
       ...
       decamt = SUM(amount*charindex(month,"Dec"))
FROM data
GROUP BY name
```

Figure 6: *A case of string base attribute.*

Here expression **charindex(month,"Jan")** plays the role of the point characteristic function for month = "Jan"; specifically, this expression returns 1 if month is "Jan" and returns 0 otherwise. (The built-in function **charindex()** attempts to match the first argument as the substring of the second one; if successful it returns the starting position of the match, else it returns zero.) Similarly for the other months. Thus, what has effectively changed here from the code of Figure 5 is the nature of the characteristic function; the rest of the code remained the same. Consequently, the problem with missing rows discussed above is still present in exactly the same form in this case as well.

Note that using a single application of **charindex()** as a characteristic function for strings has a limitation in that it will not work correctly in the presence of string values which are substrings of each other. While this does not present a problem in the above example, this limitation can easily be removed by using a product of two *symmetric* applications of **charindex()**. In our example this new, strengthened characteristic function expression for January would be **charindex(month,"Jan")*charindex("Jan",month)**. Note that this expression will work for attributes of type char(n) and also varchar(n), for any n.

4 Handling missing rows and explicit null values

We now consider a case of missing rows. We begin with the simpler case of both base and presentation attributes being numeric. Consider the statement presented in Figure 7.

```
INSERT result
SELECT name,
       janamt = MAX(amount/(1–abs(sign(month–1)))),
       febamt = MAX(amount/(1–abs(sign(month–2)))),
       ...
       decamt = MAX(amount/(1–abs(sign(month–12))))
FROM data
GROUP BY name
```

Figure 7: *Handling missing rows in case of a numeric base attribute.*

While this code uses exactly the same characteristic function as that of Figure 5, how this function is used is quite different. Here we rely on a Sybase-specific feature that division by zero returns a NULL. Thus, expression **amount/(1–abs(sign(month–1)))** returns amount only in case of January, and returns NULL otherwise. The max aggregate in turn views these NULL values as "smaller" than any real value; thus, when presented with twelve values, only one of which is really a value and the other eleven are NULL, the max aggregate would return exactly that real value.

Note that this code also works properly when presented with the case of missing data rows. Again assume that the row for Jones for February is missing. In that case, the max aggregate corresponding to the **febamt** value for Jones would be comprised of eleven components, all of which, not belonging to February, would be NULL! The max aggregate would then return NULL as the result, exactly as desired.

Finally, this code works properly if the amount values themselves are NULL. Indeed consider again the case of Jones in February, but now let this row be present but with explicit value NULL. In this case the corresponding max aggregate would be comprised of twelve values, all of which are NULL! Hence, NULL would be returned, as required.

The case of missing data rows for the string base/numeric presentation attribute combination is handled similarly, as shown in Figure 8.

```
INSERT result
SELECT name,
      janamt = MAX(amount/charindex(month,"Jan")),
      febamt = MAX(amount/charindex(month,"Feb")),
      ...
      decamt = MAX(amount/charindex(month,"Dec"))
FROM data
GROUP BY name
```

Figure 8: Handling missing rows in case of a string base attribute.

5   A special case of char(1) base attribute

While the code presented in the Sections 3 and 4 will handle base attributes of type char(1) correctly, there is in fact a simpler solution for this case. This solution, which being patterned on code in Figure 8 also handles missing data rows and explicit NULL values, is presented in Figure 9 below. (We assume here that months are represented by a single character, say 'J' for January, 'F' for February, etc., with the January/June/July, March/May and April/August conflicts having been resolved by some encoding.)

```
INSERT result
SELECT name,
      janamt = MAX(amount/(1–abs(sign(ascii(month)–ascii('J'))))),
      febamt = MAX(amount/(1–abs(sign(ascii(month)–ascii('F'))))),
      ...
      decamt = MAX(amount/(1–abs(sign(ascii(month)–ascii('D')))))
FROM data
GROUP BY name
```

Figure 9: A special case of char(1) base attribute.

The importance of this special case lies in the expected improvement in run-time efficiency, with the built-in **ascii()** function, which returns the ASCII code of its argument, being expected to be much faster than the **charindex()** function.

6 Numeric base, character presentation attributes

We now consider a sequence of cases where the presentation attribute is of string type. We start with the case of char(n) for some specific n, then consider the case of varchar(n), and finally consider a special case of char(1).

6.1 Char(n) presentation attribute

It turns out that in the case of char(n) presentation attribute the solution we have in mind requires slight individualization for every specific length n. For specificity we consider here the case of char(8). To illustrate the discussion we modify our example tables as follows: table **data** becomes **data(name, month, c8val)**, where **c8val** is of type char(8), and table **result** becomes **result(name, janc8val, febc8val, ..., decc8val)**, where **janc8val, febc8val, ..., decc8val** are again all of type char(8). Assuming that the base attribute **month** remains numeric, the pivoting code for this case is presented in Figure 10 below.

```
INSERT result
SELECT name,
       janc8val = MAX(substring(c8val,1,8*(1–abs(sign(month–1))))),
       febc8val = MAX(substring(c8val,1,8*(1–abs(sign(month–2))))),
       ...
       decc8val = MAX(substring(c8val,1,8*(1–abs(sign(month–12)))))
FROM data
GROUP BY name
```

Figure 10: Pivoting in case of presentation attribute being of type char(8).

Consider expression **substring(c8val,1,8*(1–abs(sign(month–1))))**. The subexpression **8*(1–abs(sign(month–1)))**, which uses by now familiar characteristic function for month = 1, returns 8 in case of January and returns 0 otherwise. Thus our substring expression really gets called in one of only two ways: **substring(c8val,1,8)** for January and **substring(c8val,1,0)** otherwise. In the former case the built-in function **substring()** returns the substring of **c8val** of length 8 starting at position 1— in other words **c8val** itself, and in the latter it returns NULL— exactly what is needed by the max aggregate for the correct result.

Note that this implementation again handles missing data rows and explicit NULL values. Also note that the cases of base attributes also being of string type are handled by appropriately replacing the characteristic functions involved, as shown in the previous sections.

6.2 Varchar(n) presentation attribute

We now consider the case of presentation attribute being of type varchar(n). To illustrate the discussion the tables in the example are again modified to be **data(name, month, vcval)**, where **vcval** is of type varchar(n) (for any n), and table result becomes **result(name, janvcval, febvcval, ..., decvcval)**, where **janvcval, febvcval, ..., decvcval** are again all of type varchar(n) (for the same n, of course). Assuming again that the base attribute **month** remains numeric, the pivoting code for this case is presented in Figure 11 below.

```
INSERT result
SELECT name,
       janvcval = MAX(substring(vcval,1,datalength(vcval)*
                                      (1–abs(sign(month–1))))),
       febvcval = MAX(substring(vcval,1,datalength(vcval)*
                                      (1–abs(sign(month–2))))),
       ...
       decvcval = MAX(substring(vcval,1,datalength(vcval)*
                                      (1–abs(sign(month–12)))))
FROM data
GROUP BY name
```

Figure 11: *Pivoting in case of presentation attribute being of type varchar(n).*

The difference between this case and the case of fixed-length character strings lies, of course, in the fact that we do not have a specific number to multiply our characteristic function by. Using built-in function **datalength(vcval)** which returns the actual length of the current value of attribute **vcval** solves this problem. The rest of the code remains the same. (Note that this solution works for the case of fixed-length character strings as well.)

6.3   A special case of char(1) presentation attribute

As with char(1) base attribute, there is a more efficient solution for this case as well. Assuming tables **data(name, month, c1val)** and **result(name, janc1val, febc1val, ..., decc1val)**, where **c1val** and **janc1val, febc1val, ..., decc1val** are all of type char(1), this solution is presented in Figure 12 below. (Given a valid ASCII code, built-in function **char()** converts it into a corresponding character; otherwise, it returns NULL.)

```
INSERT result
SELECT name,
       janc1val = MAX(char(ascii(c1val)/(1–abs(sign(month–1))))),
       febc1val = MAX(char(ascii(c1val)/(1–abs(sign(month–2))))),
       ...
       decc1val = MAX(char(ascii(c1val)/(1–abs(sign(month–12)))))
FROM data
GROUP BY name
```

Figure 12: *A special case of char(1) presentation attribute.*

7   Folding— inverse of pivoting

In this section we consider the problem of *table folding*, which, being the opposite of pivoting, folds short, wide tables into long, narrow ones. The conventional solution to this problem takes one insert statement for each attribute being folded. Using examples from Section 1, the code segment that folds table **result** (with numeric attribute **month**) back into table **data** is presented in Figure 13 below.

```
INSERT data
SELECT name,
      month = 1,
      amount = janamt
FROM result

INSERT data
SELECT name,
      month = 2,
      amount = febamt
FROM result

...

INSERT data
SELECT name,
      month = 12,
      amount = decamt
FROM result
```

Figure 13: A conventional solution to the table folding problem.

By employing one additional table, however, it is possible to achieve table folding in a single SQL statement. This additional table has one column, and is created manually to contain one value for each of the wide table columns to be folded. Its purpose is to in effect *split* each wide row into several narrow rows— one for each such attribute. In our example case this split table would be called **months(month)**, and would contain values 1 for **janamt,** 2 for **febamt,** etc., as shown in Figure 14.

months =

month
1
2
...
12

Figure 14: Split table for months.

Assuming that table **result** contains no NULL values, the statement which folds it into table **data** is shown in Figure 15 below. (Naturally, table **result** is now assumed to contain initial data, and table **data** is assumed to be initially empty.)

```
INSERT data
SELECT r.name,
       month = 1*(1–abs(sign(m.month–1)))+
               2*(1–abs(sign(m.month–2)))+
               ...
               12*(1–abs(sign(m.month–12))),
       amount = r.janamt*(1–abs(sign(m.month–1)))+
                r.febamt*(1–abs(sign(m.month–2)))+
                ...
                r.decamt*(1–abs(sign(m.month–12)))
FROM result r, months m
```

Figure 15: A single statement solution to the table folding problem.

By taking the cross-product of the tables, the query in effect repeats every wide row from **result** twelve times— once for each month. Consider now what happens to the January copy of the row — i.e., the one associated with the month value 1. Expression **(1–abs(sign(m.month–1)))** returns 1, and expressions **(1–abs(sign(m.month–2)))** through **(1–abs(sign(m.month–12)))** all return zeros. Thus, all but the first components of the two additive expressions in the SELECT clause are reduced to zeros, and the expressions return 1 and **r.janamt** as the values for attributes **month** and **amount** respectively. Similarly, the February copy of the row results in 2 and **r.febamt** being returned, etc.

The case of string attributes in table **data** is handled similarly. For example, in case of string representation of **month** numeric characteristic function expressions **(1–abs(sign(m.month–...)))** are replaced by appropriate string expressions as shown in Section 4, and the arithmetic expression for the value of **month** is also replaced by an appropriate string concatenation expression which reduces all but the appropriate month value to empty strings, using the techniques described in the previous sections. The case of string presentation attribute is handled in a similar way.

Note that in the absence of missing rows and NULL values in **data,** and NULL values in **result,** operations of pivoting and folding are *strict inverses* of each other, in the following sense:

(1) folding of pivoting of **data** returns exactly **data;** and
(2) pivoting of folding of **result** returns exactly **result.**

Consider, however, what happens if table **result** contains NULL amount values. First, the code of Figure 15 will no longer work. Specifically, assume that the row for Jones contains NULL for February amount. When folding it into the corresponding February narrow row, the code will generate <"Jones",2,NULL> as appropriate. But since the plus operator when applied to NULL returns NULL, it will also generate <"Jones",1,NULL> for January, <"Jones",3,NULL> for March, etc., for all months, which is incorrect.

Assuming that months remain numeric, the presence of NULL amounts in table **result** can be handled by rewriting the code as shown in Figure 16 below.

```
INSERT data
SELECT r.name,
       month = 1*(1–abs(sign(m.month–1)))+
                  2*(1–abs(sign(m.month–2)))+
                  ...
                  12*(1–abs(sign(m.month–12))),
       amount = isnull(0/(m.month–1),r.janamt)+
                  isnull(0/(m.month–2),r.febamt)+
                  ...
                  isnull(0/(m.month–12),r.decamt)
FROM result r, months m
```

Figure 16: *Folding with NULL amounts.*

Consider now what happens to the row for Jones. When folded into the February row **(m.month=2),** expressions 0/(m.month–...) for all months but February return 0, while expression 0/(m.month–2) returns NULL. Built-in function **isnull(),** which returns the first argument if it is not NULL, and the second argument otherwise, then returns 0 for the January, March, etc. components of the addition and returns **r.febamt**, which is in fact NULL, for the February component. The entire expression then returns NULL, as before.

When folded into the January row **(m.month=1)**, however, the situation changes. Now, expressions **0/(m.month–...)** for February through December return 0; thus, function **isnull()** returns 0 for all of these months, in effect neutralizing the February NULL. The January expression **0/(m.month–1)** in turn returns NULL, causing **isnull()** function to return **r.janamt**. The entire expression then returns **r.janamt,** exactly as required.

The second problem with NULL values in the **result** table is that in their presence folding no longer acts as a strict inverse of pivoting. Specifically, consider again the pivoting code of Figure 7. Whether table **data** is missing a row for Jones for February, or it has that row present with the explicit NULL value, the resulting row in the pivoted table **result** is the same: it has an explicit NULL for attribute **febamt**. Folding such a table using the technique presented in Figure 16, will on the other hand always generate the row for Jones for February with the explicit NULL in it. Thus folding cannot distinguish between the cases of missing rows and explicit NULL values for presentation attribute in the original table **data**.

8   Conclusions and related work

In this article we considered two types of information preserving table transformations: *table pivoting*— for transforming long, narrow tables into short, wide ones, and its inverse— *table folding*. The need for these transformations occurs frequently in practice, and having compact, efficient solutions for them is of importance.

Conventional SQL solutions to these problems are generally multi-statement segments of code requiring multiple passes through the data. We have presented a collection of single statement SQL solutions for these problems, considering cases of both numeric and string attributes, as well as the cases of missing rows and explicit NULL values. These solutions are not only much more compact, but are also fundamentally— often by an order of magnitude— more efficient as compared to the conventional ones. They also have an advantage of not requiring explicit transaction boundaries in order to insure proper concurrent behavior and atomicity.

Due to space limitations, in this article we limited our exposition to only some of the cases of pivoting and folding— namely, we only considered numeric and string attributes. Other data types, however, can be handled in a similar way. Datetime base and presentation attributes, for example, can be dealt with either directly by writing appropriate characteristic functions for them, or indirectly by converting them to character strings.

We also limited our examples to point-oriented pivoting, based on point characteristic functions. However, there is also a related set of interval-oriented pivoting techniques, based on interval characteristic functions, that give rise to a number of interesting and useful SQL solutions. These techniques will be presented in forthcoming articles. ❖

Effective Implementation of Conditions as Expressions in SQL Queries

David Rozenshtein, Ph.D., Anatoly Abramovich, Ph.D., and Eugene Birger, Ph.D.

reprinted from SQL Forum Journal, Vol.2, No.1, January/February 1993

1   Introduction

In this article we present techniques for effective implementation of row-level conditions as expressions that can be embedded in SQL queries. To motivate the discussion, consider a table **student_data(name, curr_yr, hs_gpa, coll_gpa)** listing student names, their current year in college (1, 2, 3, etc.) and their high school and college grade point averages. Consider also a request to compute an answer of the form **gpa_result(name, gpa),** which for every *first-year* student would list his/her high school average, and for all other students would list their college averages.

Conventional implementation of such a query is presented in Figure 1 below. As we can see, the code consists of two SQL statements, first dealing with freshmen— i.e., **curr_yr = 1**— and thus column **hs_gpa,** and the second dealing with non-freshmen— i.e., **curr_yr != 1**— and thus column **coll_gpa.**

```
INSERT gpa_result
SELECT name, gpa = hs_gpa
FROM student_data
WHERE (curr_yr = 1)

INSERT gpa_result
SELECT name, gpa = coll_gpa
FROM student_data
WHERE (curr_yr != 1)
```

Figure 1: *Conventional implementation of our query.*

Assuming that table **student_data** is clustered on **name,** each of these statements involves a pass through it, which given a large enough table is quite time consuming. The second problem with the above solution has to do with its *multistatement* nature, and becomes apparent in the context of the concurrency control and recovery issues. Indeed, to treat this as an atomic solution, one needs to surround this segment of code with transaction boundaries and appropriate commit/rollback logic. (We have also raised such a point in a similar context in [1].)

It turns out, however, that it is possible to implement this query with a *single* SQL statement, making a *single pass* through the **student_data** table. The secret of this implementation lies in properly combining our *result-contributing* columns **hs_gpa** and **coll_gpa** with the *discriminator* column **curr_yr,** in a single *discriminating expression*, which can then be used in the SELECT clause of a single resulting query.

We have developed a methodology for formulating a wide variety of such discriminating expressions. This methodology covers both numeric and non-numeric result-contributing columns, provides for alternatives among more that two such columns, and allows for use of constants and general expressions in place of them. Through proper encoding and use of the so called *characteristic functions* [2], this methodology also supports complex conditions involving discriminator columns of a variety of datatypes, as well as expressions involving them. Finally, it covers the use of discriminating expressions in SELECT, WHERE, GROUP BY and HAVING clauses of SQL queries, as well as in UPDATE statements.

In this article we illustrate this methodology by presenting solutions to a progression of problems, starting in Section 2 with our query above, and then considering several of its variations. Specifically, after introducing some notational conventions in Section 3, in Section 4 we deal with the presence of NULL values, both in the result-contributing as well as discriminator columns. In Sections 5 and 6 we look at situations where result-contributing columns are of string and datetime types. In Section 7 we consider the case of discriminating between three or more columns, and look at the *cascading IF-THEN-ELSE* formulations. In Section 8 we look at a restricted form of IF-THEN-ELSE cascades— namely the *CASE-ELSE* and *strict CASE* query forms. In Section 9 we look at an important special case of the IF-THEN-ELSE cascade, where the choice of the column is based on the first encountered non-NULL value. In Section 10 we consider the use of our discriminating expressions in the GROUP BY clause. Finally, in Section 11 we discuss their use in UPDATE statements.

While we do cover a fairly broad collection of cases in this article, due to the obvious space limitation, many other interesting cases had to be omitted. Specifically, we do not show here the use of discriminating expressions in the WHERE or HAVING clauses, and we do not consider any but the simplest conditions on numeric values. These cases will, however, be covered in forthcoming articles.

2 The case of numeric attributes

Assuming the same table **student_data** from the previous section, a single statement solution to our query is presented in Figure 2 below. (For specificity we show our examples in Sybase's Transact-SQL; however, they can also be adapted to other SQL dialects with similar features.)

```
INSERT gpa_result
SELECT name,
       gpa=hs_gpa*(1–abs(sign(curr_yr–1))) +
             coll_gpa*(abs(sign(curr_yr–1)))
FROM student_data
```

Figure 2: *A single statement solution to our query.*

The essence of this implementation lies in the fact that expression **(1–abs(sign(curr_yr–1)))** acts a *characteristic function* for **curr_yr** equal to 1. (This type of expression was also used in many of the examples of [1].) In other words, this expression returns 1 if **curr_yr** is equal to 1, and returns 0 otherwise. (Built-in function **sign()** returns –1, 0 and 1 for negative numbers, zero and positive numbers, respectively; built-in function **abs()** returns the absolute value of its argument.)

Consider now how column **gpa** is computed. Given a row with **curr_yr = 1**, expression **(1–abs(sign(curr_yr–1)))** returns 1, and expression **(abs(sign(curr_yr–1)))** returns 0. Expression for **gpa** then becomes **hs_gpa*1+coll_gpa*0,** returning column **hs_gpa** exactly as required.

Likewise, given a row with **curr_yr != 1**, expression **(1–abs(sign(curr_yr–1)))** returns 0, and expression **(abs(sign(curr_yr–1)))** returns 1. Resulting expression for **gpa** then becomes **hs_gpa*0+coll_gpa*1,** now returning column **coll_gpa,** again as required.

In concluding this section we note that the "additive" formulation used in Figure 2 is but one way of implementing discriminating expressions. In Section 4 we will present an entirely different formulation, based on the use of the **isnull()** function.

3   *Some notational conventions*

Since in this article we will be presenting a variety of problems involving the use of discriminating expressions, it turns out to be more convenient to switch to a more abstract example. (This would substantially improve readability of our SQL solutions.) Specifically, assume that the above problem is restated with respect to a table **data(name, A, B, C),** and a request is to compute the answer of the form **result(name, X),** where for every **name,** column **X** takes on either the corresponding **B** or the **C** value, depending on some condition on **A,** say **A = 1** and **A != 1,** respectively. (The nature of **A, B, C** and **X** really being immaterial.)

This would reformulate our characteristic function expression as **(1–abs(sign(A–1))),** and would restate the query as shown in Figure 3 below.

```
INSERT result
SELECT name, X = B*(1–abs(sign(A–1)))+C*(abs(sign(A–1)))
FROM data
```

Figure 3: *Restatement of the solution of Figure 2 with respect to table* **data.**

As it also turns out, we will be using the characteristic function expression (1–abs(sign(A–1))) in many examples throughout this article, so it is convenient to introduce a shorthand notation for it. Specifically, we will use expression

$$\delta[A=1]$$

to stand for the characteristic function for **A = 1**. (Naturally, in this notation any constant, or even a variable or expression, can be used in place of 1.)

The use of Greek "delta" to denote characteristic functions is an accepted convention. Intuitively, one reads this notation as "delta returns 1 if its argument is True, and returns 0 otherwise." (The square brackets are used to improve readability.) In this article we will only consider the so-called *point* characteristic functions— i.e., those based on equality— for numeric values. The same notation, however, can also be used to handle non-numeric values, as well as the so-called *interval* characteristic functions, which use <, <=, etc. operators. Techniques for encoding these functions will be presented in [2].

Noting that expression **(abs(sign(A–1))** can be rewritten as **(1–(1–abs(sign(A–1)))),** the entire expression for **X** from the statement of Figure 3 can now be rewritten as

$$X = B*\delta[A=1]+C*(1-\delta[A=1])$$

resulting in a query shown in Figure 4 below.

INSERT result
SELECT name, X = B*δ[A=1]+C*(1–δ[A=1])
FROM data

Figure 4: Restatement of the query using the "delta" notation.

4   Dealing with NULL values

Note that the solution of Figure 4 may not work correctly in the presence of NULLs in the result-contributing columns **B** and/or **C**. For example, if **A = 1,**

$B = 2$, and C is NULL, then expression for X becomes 2*1+NULL*0, and thus returns NULL as the final result. It should, however, return 2— after all, given that $A = 1$, one can argue that only the value for B should matter. Similar problem exists in the case of $A \mathrel{!}= 1$, B being NULL and C being some non-NULL value.

To handle NULLs in the result-contributing columns we modify our solution as shown in Figure 5 below.

```
INSERT result
SELECT name, X = isnull(B/δ[A=1],C/(1–δ[A=1]))
FROM data
```

Figure 5: *A single statement solution for numeric result-contributing columns with possible NULL values.*

To see how this statement works, consider what happens if $A = 1$. The characteristic function $\delta[A=1]$ then returns 1, and the expression for X becomes **isnull(B/1,C/0)**. Now, if B value itself is not NULL, then this expression evaluates to B, regardless of the value of C. (Built-in function **isnull()** returns its second argument if the first argument is NULL, and returns the first argument itself if it is not NULL.) If B value is NULL, on the other hand, then the expression returns $C/0$, which at least in Sybase, also evaluates to NULL. This resulting NULL is of course indistinguishable from the original NULL in B. To summarize, if A is 1, then X gets assigned exactly the same value as B, precisely as desired.

Consider now the case where $A \mathrel{!}= 1$. In this case, the characteristic function $\delta[A=1]$ returns 0, and the expression for X becomes **isnull(B/0,C/1)**. Since B/0 returns NULL, the **isnull()** function then returns the value of its second argument, which is of course $C/1$, or simply C. If this C is some non-NULL value, then this non-NULL value is returned; if C is NULL, then this NULL itself is returned, again completely independently from B, and again exactly as desired.

In addition to properly handling NULLs in the result-contributing columns, the above **isnull()**-based implementation of discriminating expressions also extends naturally to result-contributing columns of non-numeric types. We will show such extensions to string and datetime columns in Sections 5 and 6, respectively.

Our final example in this section deals with the situation where **A** itself can be NULL. Given a row where **A** is NULL, both solutions of Figures 4 and 5 will assign **X** to NULL, regardless of the values for **B** and **C**. While this behavior is certainly reasonable, in some situations it may prove undesirable. In that case, it can easily be modified by using expressions **isnull(δ[A=1],0)** or **isnull(δ[A=1],1)** in place of δ[A=1]. For example, rewriting expression for **X** as

$$X = isnull(B/isnull(\delta[A=1],0),C/(1-isnull(\delta[A=1],0)))$$

treats NULL **A**-values as *not being equal* to 1, and thus assigns **X** to **C** in such cases. Rewriting expression for **X** as

$$X = isnull(B/isnull(\delta[A=1],1),C/(1-isnull(\delta[A=1],1)))$$

on the other hand, treats NULL **A**-values as *being equal* to 1, and thus assigns **X** to **B** in such cases.

5 The case of string attributes

In this section we consider the case where result-contributing columns **B** and **C** are of type char(n) or varchar(n), for some n. Discriminator column **A** remains numeric, and at least for now non-NULL. We begin with the case of **B** and **C** being fixed length strings of type say char(8), length 8 being chosen arbitrarily. Solution for this case in presented in Figure 6 below.

```
INSERT result
SELECT name,
       X = isnull(substring(B,1/δ[A=1],8),
                  substring(C,1/(1–δ[A=1]),8))
FROM data
```

Figure 6: *The case of char(8) result-contributing columns* **B** *and* **C**.

Consider what happens when **A = 1**. Characteristic function δ[A=1] returns 1, and the first substring expression becomes **substring(B,1,8)**. If **B** is an actual string, then this substring expression returns a substring of **B** of length 8 starting at position 1— i.e., **B** itself. The **isnull(B,...)** expression then also returns this **B,** as appropriate. If **B** is NULL, on the other hand, the first substring expression becomes **substring(NULL,1,8)** and returns NULL. The **isnull()** function then "activates" its second argument, which becomes **substring(C,1/0,8),** or **substring(C,NULL,8),** and which returns NULL. This NULL is then returned as the final result, again as appropriate. (Note that this argument is substantially the same as the one made in discussing code of Figure 5.)

If **A!=1**, on the other hand, then characteristic function $\delta[A=1]$ returns 0, and the first substring expression becomes **substring(B,NULL,8),** and returns NULL. The **isnull()** function then returns its second argument, which is **substring(C,1,8).** This substring expression then returns **C**, regardless of whether it is an actual string or NULL, exactly as required.

The case of **B** and **C** being of type varchar(n), for some n, is handled similarly, as shown in Figure 7 below.

```
INSERT result
SELECT name,
        X = isnull(substring(B,1/δ[A=1],datalength(B)),
                    substring(C,1/(1–δ[A=1]),datalength(C)))
FROM data
```

Figure 7: *The case of varchar(n) result-contributing columns **B** and **C**.*

The only difference between this solution and the one of Figure 6 is the use of built-in function **datalength(),** which returns the length of the actual string value. (We have also discussed the use of this technique in a related context in [1].) Note that this solution also works for the case of fixed-length character strings.

Note that using the **substring()** function gives us but one way of building discriminating expressions over strings. Another interesting alternative is to use the **replicate()** function. One such solution, which works both for fixed and variable length strings, is presented in Figure 8 below.

```
INSERT result
SELECT name,
     X = isnull(replicate(B,1/δ[A=1]),replicate(C,1/(1–δ[A=1])))
FROM data
```

Figure 8: The replicate-based solution for char(n) and varchar(n) columns.

The built-in function **replicate(S,N)** returns string S concatenated with itself N times. If **A = 1**, the first invocation of **replicate()** becomes **replicate(B,1)**, and returns **B**, and the second becomes **replicate(C,NULL)**, and returns NULL. The entire expression for **X** then becomes **isnull(B,NULL)** and returns **B**, if **B** is not NULL, and NULL otherwise.

If **A != 1**, the invocations become **replicate(B,NULL)** and **replicate(C,1)**, and thus return NULL and **C** respectively. The final expression for **X** then becomes **isnull(NULL,C)** and returns **C**, again regardless of whether it is an actual string or NULL, exactly as required.

Before concluding this section, we note that the case of **A**-values being NULL is handled similarly to the way it was done in Section 4.

6   The case of datetime attributes

Given the **data** table with numeric non-NULL **A**, and columns **B** and **C** of type datetime, our query can be posed as shown in Figure 9 below.

```
INSERT result
SELECT name,
     X = isnull(dateadd(yy,0/δ[A=1],B),
                    dateadd(yy,0/(1–δ[A=1]),C))
FROM data
```

Figure 9: The case of datetime B and C.

As one can easily see, this solution has the same basic structure for the X-expression as the one of Figure 7. Consider what happens when $A = 1$. The X-expression becomes

$X = \text{isnull}(\text{dateadd}(yy,0/1,B),\text{dateadd}(yy,0/0,C))$

and thus

$X = \text{isnull}(\text{dateadd}(yy,0,B),\text{dateadd}(yy,NULL,C))$.

The first invocation of the built-in **dateadd()** function then adds 0 years to the date in **B**, and thus returns **B**; its second invocation adds NULL years to the date in **C**, and thus returns NULL. The entire expression then becomes $X = \text{isnull}(B,NULL)$, which in turns returns the value of **B**— either some real date, or NULL if that is what **B** was.

If $A \mathrel{!=} 1$, the X-expression becomes

$X = \text{isnull}(\text{dateadd}(yy,0/0,B),\text{dateadd}(yy,0/1,C))$

and thus

$X = \text{isnull}(\text{dateadd}(yy,NULL,B),\text{dateadd}(yy,0,C))$.

This in turn becomes $X = \text{isnull}(NULL,C)$, which returns the value of **C**— again, either some real date, or NULL if that is what **C** was.

In concluding this section, we note that the case of **A**-values being NULL is again handled as shown in Section 4. We also note that the choice of **yy** (year) as the first argument to the **dateadd()** function was arbitrary. Using symbols **mm** (month), **dd** (day), etc. would have given us the same effect.

7   The case of three or more result-contributing columns; or, cascading IF-THEN-ELSE formulations

In this section we consider the case of three or more result-contributing columns. Specifically, let table **data** be **data(name, A, B, C, D)** and let the query be "If **A** = 1 then **X** becomes **B**, else if **A** = 2 then **X** becomes **C**, else **X** becomes **D**." (The choice of the particular constants for **A** is of course arbitrary.) Notice that the query has the form of a *cascading IF-THEN-ELSE* statement.

Assuming numeric **A, B, C** and **D**, a general solution for this query is shown in Figure 10 below.

```
INSERT result
SELECT name,
       X = isnull(B/δ[A=1],
              isnull(C/δ[A=2],D/(1–δ[A=2]))/(1–δ[A=1]))
FROM data
```

Figure 10: *A single statement solution for the three column IF-THEN-ELSE cascade.*

Perhaps the best way to describe how this code works, is to show how it was constructed. Recall that in the two column case of Figure 5, we defined **X** as follows.

$$X = isnull(B/δ[A=1],C/(1–δ[A=1]))$$

Solution of Figure 10 was constructed simply by replacing **C** in the above expression by

$$isnull(C/δ[A=2],D/(1–δ[A=2])).$$

Since this replacement for **C** has the same structure as our original formula for **X**, all of the arguments made in Section 4 hold, and the behavior of this solution can now easily be understood. (Possible NULL **A**-values can be handled here the same way as before.)

Needless to say, this solution can be extended to any number of result-contributing columns, limited only by SQL compiler's limitation on the number of nesting levels for functions.

8 Modeling CASE statements

It is essential to note that the nested **isnull()** form used in the previous section indeed makes for a *general* solution, in the following sense. First, it can be extended to use point characteristic functions over *non-numeric* discriminator columns. (Examples of such functions were covered in [1].) Second, it can be extended to use *interval characteristic functions* (to be covered in a forthcoming article [2].) Third, conditions expressed by these characteristic functions need not be *mutually exclusive*; in other words, this solution faithfully implements conventional IF-THEN-ELSE cascades.

The query we are dealing with here, however, is actually a special case in that all of its conditions are in fact mutually exclusive. Thus except for the final ELSE clause there is, in effect, no preference order among the alternatives. In that sense, it can be viewed more restrictively as a *CASE-ELSE* statement "Case **A** of 1 return **B**; case **A** of 2 return **C**; else return **D**."

As such, assuming non-NULL **B** and **C**, this query can also be modeled as shown in Figure 11 below.

```
INSERT result
SELECT name,
       X = isnull(((isnull(0/(1–δ[A=1]),B) +
               isnull(0/(1–δ[A=2]),C))/(δ[A=1]+δ[A=2]),D)
FROM data
```

Figure 11: Implementation of CASE-ELSE formulation.

Consider the case of $A = 1$. The X-expression becomes

$$X = isnull(((isnull(0/0,B)+isnull(0/1,C))/(1+0),D)$$

which in turn becomes **X = isnull((B+0)/1,D)**, and thus **X = isnull(B,D)**, and finally returns **B**. Similarly, for **A = 2**.

If **A** is neither 1 or 2, then our X-expression becomes

X = isnull(((isnull(0/1,B)+isnull(0/1,C))/(0+0),D)

which in turn becomes **X = isnull((0+0)/0,D)**, and thus **X = isnull(NULL,D)**. This final expression of course returns **D** (whether "real" or NULL) as the result.

The case of **B** and/or **C** being NULL is handled by enhancing the above solution using a technique similar to the one used in Figure 5.

Continuing the discussion of CASE formulations, consider a somewhat different query "Case **A** of 1 return **B**; case **A** of 2 return **C**; case A of 3 return **D**." What makes this query special is that it has no ELSE clause. For such *strict CASE* queries, which in effect *require* that A takes on *exactly one* of the specified values— such situations are actually quite frequent in practice— there is a simpler form of a solution, shown in Figure 12 below.

```
INSERT result
SELECT name,
          X = isnull(0/(1–δ[A=1]),B) +
              isnull(0/(1–δ[A=2]),C) +
              isnull(0/(1–δ[A=3]),D)
FROM data
```

Figure 12: *Implementation of strict CASE formulation.*

Again, in case of **A = 1**, the **X**-expression becomes

X = isnull(0/0,B)+isnull(0/1,C)+isnull(0/1,D)

and thus **X = isnull(NULL,B)+isnull(0,C)+isnull(0,D)**, and thus returns **B**. Similarly, for **A = 2** and **A = 3**. What is interesting is that this solution also works for **B, C** and **D** values being NULL.

Our final example in this section deals with one more simplification of our implementation. It turns out that the solution of Figure 12 is fundamentally indifferent to the datatype of discriminator column **A**. The encoding of the characteristic function is of course sensitive to that, and would have to appropriately change, but this reduction of "anything" to a 1 or a 0, and the consequent "protection" of the surrounding expression from the detailed nature of the discriminator column, is precisely what characteristic functions are all about.

It also turns out that in this particular case, we can exploit the fact that column **A** is numeric, and replace a general formulation of our characteristic function by a much simpler expression designed to work specifically in this case.   In short, we can rewrite the query as shown in Figure 13 below.

```
INSERT result
SELECT name,
       X = isnull(0/(A–1),B) +
           isnull(0/(A–2),C) +
           isnull(0/(A–3),D)
FROM data
```

Figure 13: *A special simplification for strict CASE formulation for numeric* **A.**

In concluding this section we note that all of the examples presented above can be naturally extended to deal with more than three result-contributing columns.

9   When column choice is based on existence of data; or, looking for the first non-NULL value

There exists a very important special case of the IF-THEN-ELSE cascade type queries, where the column choice is not based on some "external" discriminator column, but is instead based on the existence of non-NULL values in the result-contributing columns themselves. Specifically, consider the table **data(name, A, B, C, D)** and a query "For every **name**, retrieve the corresponding **B**-value if it is not NULL, else retrieve the corresponding **C**-value if it is not NULL, else retrieve the corresponding **D**-value."

One of the solutions to this query, which is actually quite simple, is presented in Figure 14 below. (This solution was originally proposed by Dan Stone.)

```
INSERT result
SELECT name, X = isnull(B,isnull(C,D))
FROM data
```

Figure 14: *Looking for the first non-NULL value.*

Naturally this solution extends to any number of columns, subject of course to the compiler's limitation on the number of nesting levels. All one needs to do is suitably replace the second argument of the inner-most **isnull()**. For example, given a table **data(name, A, B, C, D, E)**, a query "For every **name**, retrieve the corresponding **B**-value if it is not NULL, else retrieve the corresponding **C**-value if it is not NULL, else retrieve the corresponding **D**-value if it is not NULL, else retrieve the corresponding **E**-value" is modeled by replacing the **X**-expression as follows.

$$X = isnull(B,isnull(C,isnull(D,E)))$$

10   *Using discriminating expressions in the GROUP BY clause*

All of the previous sections considered cases where discriminating expressions were used in the SELECT clause of the query. In this section we consider how such expressions can be used in the GROUP BY clause. To motivate the discussion, we go back to a "semantic" example.

Consider a table **calls(name, from_area, to_area, cost)**, where each row represents a telephone call made by a person with name **name** from the **from_area** area code to the **to_area** area code at a cost **cost**. Also consider a request to compute a table of the form **call_totals(name, call_type, total_cost)**, which would contain for each person up to two rows: the first one with the **call_type** = "local" and **total_cost** being the sum of all the calls made within the same area code, and the second, with the **call_type** = "long_dist" and the **total_cost** being the sum of all calls made between any two different area codes. (If the person made only local calls, then only the first type of row would be present in the **call_totals** table; similarly for people making only long distance calls.)

Conventional, two statement solution to the above query is shown in Figure 15 below.

```
INSERT call_totals
SELECT name, call_type = "local", total_cost = SUM(cost)
FROM calls
WHERE (from_area = to_area)
GROUP BY name

INSERT call_totals
SELECT name, call_type = "long_dist", total_cost = SUM(cost)
FROM calls
WHERE (from_area != to_area)
GROUP BY name
```

Figure 15: Conventional, two statement solution.

By incorporating an appropriate discriminating expression into a GROUP BY clause, however, it is possible to pose the above query as a single SQL statement, as shown in Figure 16 below.

```
INSERT call_totals
SELECT name,
       call_type = substring("locallong_dist",
                             isnull(1/δ[from_area=to_area],6),
                             isnull(5/δ[from_area=to_area],9)),
       total_cost = SUM(cost)
FROM calls
GROUP BY name, substring("locallong_dist",
                             isnull(1/δ[from_area=to_area],6),
                             isnull(5/δ[from_area=to_area],9))
```

Figure 16: Using a discriminating expression in the GROUP BY clause.

Before discussing how this code works, we note that in some sense it is simpler than any of the previously discussed cases. Indeed, the choice as to what will contribute to the result being made here is not even between columns, but is between string constants. This comment is of significance in that in none of the cases covered in this article one has to actually choose just between columns. One can also choose between constants, expressions or any combination thereof.

Consider now how the above code operates. Given a row, the characteristic function expression δ[from_area=to_area] returns 1 if the call was made within some single area code— i.e., **from_area** is equal to **to_area**, and returns 0 otherwise. (Given numeric **from_area** and **to_area**, such characteristic function can easily be implemented as $(1-abs(sign(from\_area-to\_area)))$.) In the former case, the **isnull()** expressions in the GROUP BY clause then become **isnull(1,6)** and **isnull(5,9)**, and thus return 1 and 5, respectively. The entire **substring** expression then becomes **substring("locallong_dist",1,5)** and returns "local". In the latter case, the **isnull()** expressions in the GROUP BY clause become **isnull(NULL,6)** and **isnull(NULL,9)**, and thus return 6 and 9, respectively. The entire **substring** expression then becomes **substring("locallong_dist",6,9)** and returns "long_dist".

Thus, for the purposes of grouping, the table in effect gets a "virtual" column **call_type**, with every row being either a "local" or a "long_dist" one. This virtual column then participates in grouping, with each person's call sums being computed separately for local and long distance calls.

In concluding this section we note that this solution can of course be extended to more than two result-contributing constants, columns, expressions, etc. Also, given that they appear in the GROUP BY clause, such discriminating expressions can also appear in the HAVING clause as well. Finally, the substring extraction technique underlying this solution is very interesting in and of itself, and can be used quite effectively in many different situations.

11 Using discriminating expressions in the UPDATE statements

Note that all of the discriminating expressions presented in this article can also be used in the SET clause of an UPDATE statement. This is of extreme importance, since updates often require passes through the table being updated. Thus, given an update involving such a discrimination, the difference between our single-statement implementation and the conventional multi-statement implementation becomes that much more dramatic.

12 Conclusion

In this article we have presented an approach for effective implementation of *row-level* conditions as *discriminating expressions* in SQL queries, and have shown how such expressions can then be embedded in the SELECT and GROUP BY clauses. The primary significance of our approach is that it provides a means for formulating many types of questions, which would conventionally be implemented as a sequence of several SQL statements, as a single SQL statement.

Due to the obvious space limitations, not all of the cases covered by our approach could be presented in this article. Notably, we have omitted examples showing the use— and particularly peculiarities of this use— of discriminating expressions in the WHERE and HAVING clauses. These cases, however, will be presented in forthcoming articles.

Finally, we note that issues raised in this article have nothing to do with the *control flow* level IF-ELSE construct of Transact-SQL.

References

[1] D. Rozenshtein, A. Abramovich, E. Birger. "Single Statement SQL Solutions to the Table Pivoting and Folding Problems." In *SQL Forum Journal*, 1(12), November/December 1992.
[2] D. Rozenshtein, A. Abramovich, E. Birger. "Encoding and Use of Characteristic Functions in SQL." In *SQL Forum Journal*, 2(2), March/April 1993
❖

Encoding and Use of Characteristic Functions in SQL

David Rozenshtein, Ph.D., Anatoly Abramovich, Ph.D., and Eugene Birger, Ph.D.

reprinted from SQL Forum Journal, Vol.2, No.2, March/April 1993

1 Introduction

In this article we describe a conceptual device, called a *characteristic function*, and show how these characteristic functions can be encoded and used in SQL, often dramatically improving compactness and efficiency of the resulting code.

Functionally, characteristic functions are devices for recognizing conditions, which take Boolean expressions as arguments and convert them to numeric results. Syntactically, they are traditionally expressed using the following "delta"-notation

$$\delta[\alpha]$$

where α is some Boolean expression. (The square brackets around the argument are used to improve readability.)

Semantically, their behavior is defined as follows: Expression $\delta[\alpha]$ returns 1 if its argument α evaluates to True, returns 0 if α evaluates to False, and returns NULL if α evaluates to NULL. For example, expression $\delta[A=35]$, where A is some attribute from some table, returns 1 for those rows where A is in fact equal to 35, 0 for rows with A equal to some other value, and NULL for rows with A being NULL.

Structurally, characteristic functions are implemented (encoded) as expressions, using the basic operators of the SQL language, as well as the built-in functions provided by it. The exact nature of these implementations varies widely among SQL dialects, as it depends greatly on the extent of the built-in facilities provided by the language. Furthermore, it is often the case that even within the same

SQL dialect, formulating characteristic function expressions for values of some data types is significantly easier that for some others.

As an example of an actual implementation of a characteristic function, consider expression

$$1-abs(sign(A-35))$$

which, as can be shown by a simple trace, serves as a proper encoding for our example function $\delta[A=35]$. Other implementations are of course also possible. For example, expression

$$isnull(0/(A-35),1-A*0)$$

serves as a proper encoding for $\delta[A=35]$ as well. (Definitions of built-in functions **sign()**, **abs()** and **isnull()** are presented in the next section.)

It is precisely their combined ability to act as *condition evaluators*, but to present themselves as *expressions*, that makes characteristic functions the extremely powerful and versatile devices that they are. Indeed, we have developed an entire relational implementation methodology for solving a wide variety of problems based on the use of these characteristic functions. This methodology has provided us with substantial— often an order of magnitude— speed-ups for many solutions. It has also allowed us to formulate efficient loop-free single-statement SQL solutions for some very difficult problems, where conventional solutions traditionally involved row-at-a-time processing and the use of explicit loops. Finally, it has provided us with an approach to embedding program logic conventionally implemented in the control structures of the host language directly into the SQL statements themselves, resulting in some very interesting possibilities.

We have already reported some of the results of this work in [1,2] and will continue doing so in the forthcoming articles. In [1] we have shown how to build single-statement SQL solutions to the so called *table pivoting* and *folding* problems— e.g., how to transform table **salary1(name, month, amt)** to table **salary2(name, jan_amt, feb_amt, ..., dec_amt)** and *vice versa*. These single-statement solutions are substantially more efficient than their conventional multi-statement counterparts.

In [2] we solved a completely different kind of problem; specificaly, we showed how by implementing row-level conditions as expressions, we can then place them into SELECT, GROUP BY and SET clauses of SQL statements, again resulting in dramatic improvements in efficiency. A typical problem which can be solved by this technique is: How, by making just *one pass* through a table, to *conditionally* update *several* columns, even though each column has its own, different from others, update condition.

While both [1,2] contained many examples of characteristic functions, the goal of those articles was to describe solutions for specific classes of problems. In this article, on the other hand, we concentrate on presenting the characteristic functions themselves. Indeed, we have developed a systematic approach to the encoding of characteristic functions in SQL. We begin with presenting a system of such functions for numeric expressions, continue with expressions of datetime type, and finally consider the character strings. In doing so, we consider characteristic functions over full three-valued logic, and over full set of binary comparators, as well as over NULLs.

We illustrate the discussion with several examples showing how to effectively implement a certain class of queries, called *horizontal histograms*, as single SQL statements. While interesting and indeed useful in and of themselves, in some sense these histogram examples are also the simplest kinds of characteristic function applications, and as such allow us to concentrate on the systematic presentation of characteristic functions themselves.

2   Encoding characteristic functions for numeric expressions

The system of characteristic functions for numeric expressions consists of eight *simple characteristic functions*— one for each of the binary comparators: =, !=, <, etc., as well as for IS NULL and IS NOT NULL operators, and three *derivation rules* for each of the logical operators: NOT, AND and OR.

Figure 1 below presents one possible encoding for such a system. (For specificity, in this article we cast all of our code examples in Transact-SQL of Sybase. Also, as long as they remain numeric, symbols **A** and **B** can stand for attributes from some table or tables, or they can be constants, variables or even general expressions. Symbols α and β represent logical expressions.)

$$\delta[A=B] = 1-abs(sign(A-B))$$
$$\delta[A!=B] = abs(sign(A-B))$$
$$\delta[A<B] = 1-sign(1+sign(A-B))$$
$$\delta[A<=B] = sign(1-sign(A-B))$$
$$\delta[A>B] = 1-sign(1-sign(A-B))$$
$$\delta[A>=B] = sign(1+sign(A-B))$$
$$\delta[A\ IS\ NULL] = isnull(0*A,1)$$
$$\delta[A\ IS\ NOT\ NULL] = 1-isnull(0*A,1)$$

$$\delta[NOT\ \alpha] = 1-\delta[\alpha]$$
$$\delta[\alpha\ AND\ \beta] = isnull(\delta[\alpha]*\delta[\beta],\ 0/(1-isnull(\delta[\alpha],1)*isnull(\delta[\beta],1)))$$
$$\delta[\alpha\ OR\ \beta] = isnull(sign(\delta[\alpha]+\delta[\beta]),\ 1/(isnull(\delta[\alpha],0)+isnull(\delta[\beta],0)))$$

Figure 1: *A system of characteristic functions for numeric expressions.*

The rest of this section is organized as follows. First, we discuss the encodings for the three basic characteristic functions: $\delta[A=B]$, $\delta[A<B]$ and $\delta[A\ IS\ NULL]$. We then introduce the notion of *three-valued logic*, and show how the other five simple characteristic functions from Figure 1 can be derived from the three basic ones using the NOT derivation rule. We then discuss the other two derivation rules. Finally, we consider an important class of *bounded interval* characteristic functions, and show how such functions can be derived from the above system.

Consider expression

$$\delta[A=B] = 1-abs(sign(A-B))$$

which is, of course, a generalization of the example encoding from the previous section. If **A** is indeed equal to **B**, then **A–B** is 0, **sign()** returns 0, **abs()** returns 0, and the entire expression returns 1, as required. (Built-in function **sign()** returns –1, 0 and +1 for negative numbers, zero and positive numbers respectively. Built-in function **abs()** returns the absolute value of its argument.) If **A** is not equal to **B**, on the other hand, then **A–B** returns some non-zero result, **sign()**

returns either −1 or +1, **abs()** returns +1, and the entire expression returns 0, again exactly as required. Finally, if **A** and/or **B** are NULL, both the **sign()** and the **abs()** functions return NULL, and the entire expression also returns NULL. This is appropriate, since it is consistent with the basic behavior of binary comparator =.

Consider now expression

$$\delta[A<B] = 1-\text{sign}(1+\text{sign}(A-B))$$

If **A<B**, then the inner **sign()** returns −1, the argument to the outer **sign()** becomes 0, the outer **sign()** returns 0, and the entire expression returns 1. On the other hand, if **A>B**, then the inner **sign()** returns +1, the argument to the outer **sign()** becomes 2, the outer **sign()** returns +1, and the entire expression returns 0. Likewise, if **A=B**, then **A–B** returns 0, the inner **sign()** returns 0, the outer **sign()** returns +1, and the entire expression again returns 0. Finally, if **A** and/or **B** are NULL, the entire expression also returns NULL, again in a manner consistent with the basic behavior of <.

Finally, consider expression

$$\delta[A \text{ IS NULL}] = \text{isnull}(0*A,1)$$

Here, if **A** is in fact **NULL**, expression **0*NULL** returns **NULL**, and expression **isnull(NULL,1)** returns 1 as the final result. (Built-in function **isnull()** returns its first argument if it is not NULL, and returns its second argument otherwise.) If **A** is not **NULL**, on the other hand, then **0*A** returns 0, which is then returned as the final result.

Before proceeding further, we note that in order to stay consistent with Sybase, all of the derivation rules in our characteristic system must be evaluated in the context of the so called *three-valued logic*, where result of a logical expression can be False, True or NULL (sometimes referred to as Maybe). Semantics of this three-valued logic is defined by the truth tables presented in Figure 2 below. (Here, symbols **F, N** and **T** stand for False, NULL and True, respectively.)

NOT	F	N	T
	T	N	F

AND	F	N	T
F	F	F	F
N	F	N	N
T	F	N	T

OR	F	N	T
F	F	N	T
N	N	N	T
T	T	T	T

Figure 2: *Truth tables for the three-valued logic.*

Consider now the NOT derivation rule from Figure 1. As one can easily see, it is consistent with the NOT truth table above. Given such a rule, the rest of the simple characteristic functions in our system can be derived from the basic three, as follows. Expression $\delta[A!=B]$ can be derived as $1-\delta[A=B]$, expression $\delta[A>=B]$ as $1-\delta[A<B]$, and expression $\delta[A \text{ IS NOT NULL}]$ as $1-\delta[A \text{ IS NULL}]$. Also, given that $\text{sign}(A-B) = -\text{sign}(B-A)$, we have

$$\delta[A>B] = \delta[B<A] = 1-\text{sign}(1+\text{sign}(B-A)) = 1-\text{sign}(1-\text{sign}(A-B))$$

Finally, expression $\delta[A<=B]$ can be derived as $1-\delta[A>B]$.

Consider now the AND derivation rule from Figure 1.

$$\delta[\alpha \text{ AND } \beta] = \text{isnull}(\delta[\alpha]*\delta[\beta], 0/(1-\text{isnull}(\delta[\alpha],1)*\text{isnull}(\delta[\beta],1)))$$

This rule returns an obviously correct 0 or 1 if neither α nor β are NULL. If at least one of them is NULL, then expression $\delta[\alpha]*\delta[\beta]$ returns NULL, and the control passes to the second argument of the outer **isnull()** function, which in turn returns 0 if one of α and β is False and the other is NULL, and returns NULL otherwise, all in accordance with the AND truth table.

The OR derivation rule is reasoned out in substantially the same fashion.

It is interesting to note that, if we were dealing with two valued logic (i.e., no NULL truth values), or if it was guaranteed that the only way α and β could be NULL, is to be NULL *simultaneously*, then we could substantially simplify our AND and OR derivation rule expressions as shown in Figure 3 below. (The NOT derivation rule remains the same.)

$$\delta[\alpha \text{ AND } \beta] \quad = \delta[\alpha]*\delta[\beta]$$
$$\delta[\alpha \text{ OR } \beta] \quad = \text{sign}(\delta[\alpha]+\delta[\beta])$$

Figure 3: *The AND and OR derivation rules for two valued logic, or for the case where α and β can only be NULL simultaneously.*

We now consider an interesting class of characteristic functions that can be derived from the above system. Specifically, consider the function $\delta[A<X<=B]$, for numeric **A, B** and **X**. This function, which in effect defines a *bounded interval* for **X**, can be restated as

$$\delta[A<X<=B] = \delta[(A<X) \text{ AND } (X<=B)]$$

and thus can be fully expanded into a regular arithmetic expression using the AND derivation rule from Figure 1 and the encodings for $\delta[A<X]$ and $\delta[X<=B]$.

Unfortunately, this expansion is quite bulky (although, and this must be emphasized, it still perfectly legal and functional.) It is also often an "overkill" in the sense that it works for *any* combination of **A, B** and **X**. In many practical situations, however, one can rely on the range boundaries **A** and **B** *not* being NULL. In such a cases, a much simpler definition, based on the AND rule of Figure 3, is possible.

$$\delta[A<X<=B] = \delta[A<X]*\delta[X<=B] = (1-\text{sign}(1+\text{sign}(A-X)))*\text{sign}(1-\text{sign}(X-B))$$

Finally, in many situations one can make a further simplifying assumption that the interval is in fact "proper"— i.e., **A<=B**. (Note, this requires that **A** and **B** be non-NULL.) In this case, we can simplify our expressions even further. Specifically, consider the following expression.

$$\delta[A<X<=B] = \delta[A<X] - \delta[B<X]$$

To see how this works, consider some **A, B** and **X**, such that **X** is not NULL, and **A<X<=B**. Now, since **A<X**, $\delta[A<X]$ returns 1. Since **X<=B**, $\delta[B<X]$ which tests the condition exactly opposite to **X<=B**, returns 0. The entire expression then returns 1, as desired. Now consider the two remaining cases. First, let

X<=A. Then, A<X returns False; by that and by A<=B, B<X returns False; both δ[A<X] and δ[B<X] return 0; and the final result returns 0, as desired. Alternatively, let B<X. Now, B<X returns True; by that and by A<=B, A<X returns True; both δ–expressions return 1; and the final result again returns 0. Finally, if X is NULL, then the entire expression δ[A<X<=B] also returns NULL.

By expanding the δ–expressions in the above definition, we get a very manageable:

$$\delta[A<X<=B] = \text{sign}(1+\text{sign}(B–X)) – \text{sign}(1+\text{sign}(A–X))$$

The other three bounded interval cases δ[A<X<B], δ[A<=X<B] and δ[A<=X<=B] are implemented in a similar fashion. (Note that the last of these δ–expressions implements standard BETWEEN operator.)

3 Examples of histogram implementations using characteristic functions

In this section we present a series of examples illustrating the use of numeric characteristic functions. Specifically we show how one can conveniently and efficiently pose a wide variety of *horizontal histogram*-type questions as single SQL statement queries. Interestingly, techniques presented in this section also rely upon, as well as extend, the solution to the table pivoting problem presented in [1].

As we have pointed out earlier, while interesting and useful in and of themselves, histograms also provide us with one of the "purest" applications of characteristic functions. Indeed, all that we effectively do in histograms is mark the rows with 1's or 0's for the inclusion in various counts, based on some conditions. (Many other, much more complex examples of the effective use of characteristic functions are possible. Some have already been presented in [1,2]; others will be presented in the forthcoming articles.)

Consider now a table **employee(emp#, name, age, sal, dept, kids)**, with **emp#** being a key, which lists for every employee his/her employee number, name, age, salary, department he/she is in, and the number of children he/she has (which can be 0, 1, 2, etc.)

Consider also a request to compute a table of the form **histogram1(no_kids, one_kid, many_kids, unknown_kids)**, listing how many employees have zero, one, or more children, or for whom the number of children is unknown— i.e., NULL. (Note that the answer to this query should be a single data row.)

A single SQL statement query posing this request is shown in Figure 4 below. (For clarity, we intentionally present our queries in a compact δ–notation. Naturally, one has to fully expand all δ–expressions before using this solution in actual code.)

```
INSERT histogram1
SELECT no_kids        = SUM(δ[kids=0]),
       one_kid        = SUM(δ[kids=1]),
       many_kids      = SUM(1–δ[kids=0] – δ[kids=1]),
       unknown_kids   = SUM(δ[kids IS NULL])
FROM employee
```

Figure 4: *A point-oriented histogram of number of children.*

To understand how this code works, observe that every row from table **employee** contributes to exactly one sum, thus in effect making the sums act like mutually exclusive counters. For example, a row with **kids=0**, has δ[kids=0] evaluate to 1 and the other two δ–expressions— for 1 and for IS NULL— evaluate to 0. Thus, this row is counted in the sum for **no_kids**, and is not counted in any other sum. Similarly, for rows with **kids** value of 1.

For a row with **kids** value 2 or more, in turn, all three of the δ–expressions in this query evaluate to 0. Thus, this row does not contribute to either of the first two sums, or to the sum for **unknown_kids**, and instead contributes only to the third sum for **many_kids**, where expression **1–δ[kids=0]–δ[kids=1]** of course returns 1.

Finally, a row with **kids** value of NULL has both of the δ–expressions for 0 and 1 evaluate to NULLs, which are then ignored by the sum function in the first three sums, and δ[kids IS NULL] evaluate to 1. Thus, this row contributes only to the last sum for **unknown_kids**.

Before proceeding further, we note that a conventional implementation of this query would require 4 statements, each computing one of the resulting counts, and as we have argued in [1], would be substantially less efficient. We also note that, should *every row* in table **employee** contain NULL value for **kids**, results of the first three sums in the SELECT clause would also return NULL. If this is undesirable, one can easily convert these NULLs to zeros by surrounding them as follows: **isnull(SUM(...),0).**

Given the same table **employee**, consider now a request to compute a histogram of the form **histogram2(less_10K, between_10K_50K, more_50K, unknown_sal)**, counting how many employees have a salary within a specified interval.

A solution to this request is shown in Figure 5 below. (The reasoning behind this code is substantially the same as the one for the previous example.)

```
INSERT histogram2
SELECT less_10K          = SUM(δ[sal<10,000]),
       between_10K_50K   = SUM(δ[10,000<=sal<50,000]),
       more_50K          = SUM(δ[50,000<=sal]),
       unknown_sal       = SUM(δ[sal IS NULL])
FROM employee
```

Figure 5: *An interval-oriented histogram of salary ranges.*

We now consider some of the variations on these histograms. First, consider a request to compute a histogram for the number of children, but now not for the entire table, but rather by department. Assuming a suitably defined result table, all that one has to do is modify the solution of Figure 4 as shown in Figure 6 below. (To make the example more compact, we also use here the equivalent, interval-oriented δ[kids>=2] in computing the sum for **many_kids.**)

A much more interesting, and complex variation, is to compute a histogram of salary ranges based on age ranges, say for employees younger than 30, those between 30 and 60, and those over 60. (Histograms of this kind, which are often called "stratified", are an important tool in comparative statistical analysis.

Indeed, this very example might serve as a useful query in testing for possible age discrimination.)

```
INSERT histogram3
SELECT dept,
        no_kids          = SUM(δ[kids=0]),
        one_kid          = SUM(δ[kids=1]),
        many_kids        = SUM(δ[kids>=2]),
        unknown_kids     = SUM(δ[kids IS NULL])
FROM employee
GROUP BY dept
```

Figure 6: A histogram of number of children by department.

Assume then result table of the form **histogram4(age_group, less_10K, between_10K_50K, more_50K, unknown_salary)**, where **age_group** is a string with intended values "y" (young), "m" (middle aged), "o" (old), and "u" (age unknown, i.e., NULL). A solution to this request is shown in Figure 7 below.

```
INSERT histogram4
SELECT
    age_group =
        substring("ymou",1*isnull(δ[age<30],0)+
                          2*isnull(δ[30<=age<60],0)+
                          3*isnull(δ[60<=age],0)+
                          4*δ[age IS NULL],1),
    less_10K             = SUM(δ[sal<10,000]),
    between_10K_50K      = SUM(δ[10,000<=sal<50,000]),
    more_50K             = SUM(δ[50,000<=sal]),
    unknown_sal          = SUM(δ[sal IS NULL])

FROM employee
GROUP BY substring("ymou",1*isnull(δ[age<30],0)+
                           2*isnull(δ[30<=age<60],0)+
                           3*isnull(δ[60<=age],0)+
                           4*δ[age IS NULL],1)
```

Figure 7: A histogram of salary ranges by age groups.

The difference between this code and the code of Figure 5 is, of course, the substring expression used in the SELECT and the GROUP BY clauses. To understand how this expression works, consider some row from table **employee** with **age** value, say, 25. Given this row, δ[age<30] returns 1, and all other δ–expressions return 0. The substring expression then becomes

substring("ymou",1*1+2*0+3*0+4*0,1)

and thus **substring("ymou",1,1)**, which then returns a substring of its first argument of length 1 starting at position 1— i.e, "y"— as the result.

Likewise, given a row with **age** value, say, 40, δ[30<=age<60] returns 1, and all other δ–expressions return 0. The substring expression then becomes **substring("ymou",2,1)**, and returns "m" as the result. Similarly, for rows with **age** value 60 or more.

Finally, consider a row with **age** value NULL. Here δ[age **IS NULL**] returns 1, and all other δ–expressions return NULL. These NULLs, however, are then immediately turned into zeros by the **isnull()** function. Thus, the substring expression becomes **substring("ymou",4,1)**, and returns "u" as the result.

Thus, for the purposes of grouping, each of the rows acquires one of the four pre-specified **age_group** values: "y", "m", "o" and "u", and falls into the corresponding group. The salary histogram is then computed for each of the groups separately.

Before concluding this section, we note that in both of the solutions of Figure 5 and 7, all bounded intervals for **age** and **salary** are in fact proper. This in turn permits the use of the simpler expansion, described at the end of the previous section, of the δ–expressions involved. We also note that the solution of Figure 7 is based, to a great extent, on the technique for using characteristic functions in the GROUP BY clause first described in [2], where we also show techniques that can be used to extend age group identifies to their full names— e.g., "young", "middle aged", etc. Finally, as was shown in Figure 5, one can mix in the same histogram point and interval oriented conditions; furthermore, the conditions defining the histogram counts need not be mutually exclusive.

4 Encoding characteristic functions for datetime expressions

In this section we show how one can define a system of characteristic functions for datetime expressions. Consider expression **datediff(ms,D2,D1)**. This expression, which uses a built-in function **datediff()**, returns a difference, in milliseconds, between two datetime quantities **D1** and **D2**. (Again, **D1** and **D2** can be attributes, variable, constants of expressions of type datetime.) Specifically, for **D1=D2** it returns 0, for **D1<D2** it returns a negative number, and for **D1>D2** it returns a positive number.

In other words, **datediff(ms,D2,D1)** does to the datetime **D1** and **D2** exactly what expression **A–B** did for numeric **A** and **B**— i.e., differentiate between the less than, the greater than, and the equality cases. This in turn suggests the following definitions for the two basic non-NULL characteristic functions.

$$\delta[D1=D2] = 1-abs(sign(datediff(ms,D2,D1)))$$
$$\delta[D1<D2] = 1-sign(1+sign(datediff(ms,D2,D1)))$$

Unfortunately, this does not always work, as the result of **datediff()** is defined to be of type integer, and the application of **datediff(ms,D2,D1)** expression to **D1** and **D2** differing by more than approximately 24 days simply results in an overflow.

It seems that it should be possible to compensate for this, by using the following two-step process to compare datetime values. The first step compares the values at granularity of days— there is no danger of overflow here— returning negative, positive or zero result, as appropriate. The second step, which is invoked only if the first step returns zero, compares the values at granularity of milliseconds within that day. This then suggests replacing our simple **datediff()** expression in the above δ–expressions as follows. (Symbol **dd** is the appropriate first argument here.)

$$isnull(1.0/datediff(dd,D2,D1),datediff(ms,D2,D1))$$

Unfortunately, and this we consider a flaw on the part of Sybase, this does not work either. The problem is that Sybase computes **datediff(ms,D2,D1)** *before* it is determined that the computation would actually be invoked by the **isnull()** function. Thus, the same overflow problem is still present.

A workaround here is to encode the **isnull()** expression as follows.

```
isnull(1.0/datediff(dd,D2,D1),
        datediff(ms,convert(char(8),D1,112),D1)–
        datediff(ms,convert(char(8),D2,112),D2))
```

Here expression **convert(char(8),D1,112)** computes a datetime value which is the *exact midnight* of the day corresponding to **D1**. (Third argument 112 is the appropriate control code for Sybase's built-in function **convert()**.) Expression **datediff(ms,convert(char(8),D1,112),D1)** then computes the offset, in milliseconds, between the exact time point **D1**, and **D1**'s midnight. (It should be pointed out, however, that Sybase's granularity of time is 1/300-th of a second.) Similarly, for the second **datediff(ms,...)** expression. Expression **datediff(ms,...)** – **datediff(ms,...)** then properly compares **D1** and **D2**, without any danger of overflow.

The final expressions for the two basic non-NULL characteristic functions for datetime expressions then become

$$\delta[D1=D2] = 1-\text{abs}(\text{sign}(\text{isnull}(1.0/\text{datediff}(dd,D2,D1),$$
$$\text{datediff}(ms,\text{convert}(char(8),D1,112),D1)-$$
$$\text{datediff}(ms,\text{convert}(char(8),D2,112),D2)$$
$$)))$$

$$\delta[D1<D2] = 1-\text{sign}(1+\text{sign}(\text{isnull}(1.0/\text{datediff}(dd,D2,D1),$$
$$\text{datediff}(ms,\text{convert}(char(8),D1,112),D1)-$$
$$\text{datediff}(ms,\text{convert}(char(8),D2,112),D2)$$
$$)))$$

The basic NULL-recognizing characteristic function for datetime quantities is defined as follows.

$$\delta[D \text{ IS NULL}] = \text{isnull}(0*\text{datepart}(yy,D),1)$$

Here, the built-in function **datepart(yy,D)** extracts years from datetime **D**. If **D** is some real date, then this function returns its year component (as a number); if **D** is NULL, then it returns NULL. (The use of **yy** to extract years from **D** here is arbitrary; arguments **mm, dd**— for month, day— etc. can also be used.) The **isnull()** function then returns 0 or 1, respectively.

Given the three basic characteristic function encodings above, the rest of the characteristic system for datetime quantities— notably, including bounded interval functions— can be build using the three derivation rules in exactly the same way as it was done for numerics.

5 *Universal system of characteristic functions*

As we have in effect argued, the characteristic function systems for numeric and datetime quantities differ in exactly two places: (1) which expression was used as the argument to the inner-most **sign()** function in the first six δ–expressions of Figure 1; and (2) which expression was used as the first argument in the **isnull()** function of the two NULL-recognizing δ–expressions there.

This observation allows us to view our characteristic system of Figure 1 as *universally applicable* to any data type, as long as the following holds. First, given two quantities **Arg1** and **Arg2** of that data type, we can define differentiating expression $\Delta(\textbf{Arg1},\textbf{Arg2})$ to return some negative numeric value if **Arg1<Arg2**, some positive numeric value if **Arg1>Arg2**, zero if **Arg1=Arg2**, and NULL if one or both of **Arg1** and **Arg2** are NULL. (Operators < and > here must, of course, have meaning appropriate to the data type of **Arg1** and **Arg2**.) Second, given **Arg** of that same data type, we also can define expression $\Gamma(\textbf{Arg})$ to return NULL if **Arg** is NULL, and some non-NULL numeric value otherwise.

Given such encodings for these Δ– and Γ– expressions for some data type, we can now define our three basic characteristic functions for that data type as follows.

$$\delta[\text{Arg1}=\text{Arg2}] \quad = 1-\text{abs}(\text{sign}(\Delta(\text{Arg1},\text{Arg2})))$$
$$\delta[\text{Arg1}<\text{Arg2}] \quad = 1-\text{sign}(1+\text{sign}(\Delta(\text{Arg1},\text{Arg2})))$$
$$\delta[\text{Arg IS NULL}] \quad = \text{isnull}(0*\Gamma(\text{Arg}),1)$$

6   Encoding characteristic functions for strings

Given the universal expressions from the previous section, all we need to do in order to define a system of characteristic functions for strings, is to encode expressions for $\Delta(S1,S2)$ and $\Gamma(S)$, where S1, S2 and S are of string type.

The Γ–expression presents no problem, e.g., it can be defined as **ascii(S)** for S of type char(n) or varchar(n) for any n, giving

$$\delta[S\ IS\ NULL] = isnull(0*ascii(S),1)$$

Here, built-in function **ascii()** returns the ASCII code of the first character of S if S is some non-empty string, return the ASCII code of space if S is the empty string, and returns NULL if S is NULL.

The difficulty lies in the general Δ–expression. As it turns out, Sybase currently lacks sufficient built-in facilities to define a single, universally applicable $\Delta(S1,S2)$ expression for alphabetic comparison that would work for arguments of type char(n) and varchar(n) for all n. What is possible, however, is to define such Δ–expressions for fixed-length strings of a particular length. For example, for type char(1), one possible encoding is as follows.

$$\Delta(S1,S2) = ascii(S1) - ascii(S2)$$

For type char(3), it is as follows. (Symbols $\sigma1$, $\sigma2$ and $\sigma3$ are ancillary definitions which, of course, have to be completely expanded in the actual code. Without them, however, the code below becomes quite difficult to read, as its essence simply gets lost in the detail.)

$$\Delta(S1,S2) = isnull(1.0/\sigma1,isnull(1.0/\sigma2,\sigma3))$$

where

$\sigma1 = ascii(S1)-ascii(S2)$
$\sigma2 = ascii(substring(S1,2,1))-ascii(substring(S2,2,1))$
$\sigma3 = ascii(substring(S1,3,1))-ascii(substring(S2,3,1))$

This encoding, which uses the nested **isnull()** technique described in [2], in effect compares **S1** and **S2** *lexicographically*, one character at a time, left to right. As we have also noted in [2], this solution can be extended to any length n, limited only by Sybase's limitations on the number of nesting levels for functions. As such, we can use it to define characteristic function systems for char(n) and varchar(n) for quite a few values of n. (Variable-length strings can be easily handled here by converting them to fixed-length).

Admittedly, we do find this solution awkward, particularly in light of the fact that not much in terms of built-in facilities is actually necessary to enable a compact universal definition of Δ–expression for alphabetic comparison of strings, and also given that many other systems do provide such facilities. For example, the Microsoft Access system has a built-in function **StrComp()**, which returns –1, +1 and 0 for <, > and = comparisons of strings, respectively— i.e., exactly what we need. Oracle, while not being so convenient, still provides function **greatest()**, which when invoked for two strings returns the lexicographically larger of the two; this, it turns out, is also sufficient for our purposes. What Sybase gives us is a built-in function **difference(S1,S2)**; however, this function computes the difference between the SOUNDEX values of the two strings, and as such is completely inappropriate for our purpose.

Finally, we note that by going outside of our universal framework for defining characteristic functions, we can in fact define the basic equality-recognizing characteristic function δ[S1=S2], for strings of type char(n) or varchar(n) for any n, as follows.

$$\delta[S1=S2] = charindex(S1,S2)*charindex(S2,S1)$$

This definition, first introduced in [1], uses Sybase's built-in function **charindex()** which attempts to match its first argument as the substring of the second; if successful, it returns the starting position of the match, else it returns 0. Thus, if **S1**=**S2**, then both invocations of **charindex()** return 1, and the δ–expression also returns 1. If **S1**!=**S2**, then at least one of the invocations returns 0, and the δ–expression also returns 0. (The two symmetric applications of **charindex()** are necessary to handle cases where one of the strings is the proper prefix of the other.) Finally, if one of **S1** or **S2** is NULL, then the entire expression also returns NULL. Using this definition and the NOT derivation rule, we can also define δ[S1!=S2] in a natural manner.

7 Conclusion

In this article we have described a conceptual device, called a *characteristic function*, and have presented a systematic approach to the encoding of these functions for numeric, datetime and string expressions, accounting for full three-valued logic and for NULL values. The importance of characteristic functions lies in the fact that they allow logical conditions to be treated as numeric expressions, and as such permit the embedding of these conditions into SELECT, GROUP BY, SET, etc., clauses of SQL statements. This, in turn, often leads to dramatically more compact and efficient solutions to many classes of important practical problems.

This article is a third in a series of articles describing a relational implementation methodology based on the use of these characteristic functions. Previously, in [1,2], we have shown how these functions can be used to efficiently solve the so called table *pivoting* and *folding* problems, and how to implement row-level *if-then-else* type questions as single SQL queries. In this article we have shown how they can be used to support single statement implementations of a certain class of queries called *horizontal histograms*, both for discrete as well as interval conditions. Other uses of characteristic functions will be presented in the forthcoming articles.

References

[1] D. Rozenshtein, A. Abramovich, E. Birger. "Single Statement SQL Solutions to the Table Pivoting and Folding Problems." In *SQL Forum Journal*, 1(12), November-December 1992.
[2] D. Rozenshtein, A. Abramovich, E. Birger. "Effective Implementation of Conditions as Expressions in SQL Queries." In *SQL Forum Journal*, 2(1), January-February 1993.

The Power of Self-Joins: SQL Solutions to the Median and Other Row Positioning Problems

David Rozenshtein, Ph.D., Anatoly Abramovich, Ph.D.,
Yelena Alexandrova, and Eugene Birger, Ph.D.

reprinted from SQL Forum Journal, Vol.2, No.4, July/August 1993

1 Introduction

In this article we show how *self-joins* synergistically combine with *characteristic functions* [6,7,8] to provide compact SQL solutions to a wide variety of the so called *row positioning* problems. These problems, which are most naturally stated in terms of conditions on *where*— i.e., in which positions— the data rows should lie in a sorted data sequence, include some extremely important data processing operations such as, for example, finding medians, or splitting ordered sequences into several contiguous subsequences.

What makes these problems all the more interesting is their fundamental "anti-relational" nature. Indeed, due to their basic positional formulation, these problems have always been conventionally solved by sorting and then sequentially processing the data, with SQL-based solutions generally employing cursors over ORDER BY queries. (In Transact SQL, it is also possible to achieve this using the **SET rowcount 1** technique and a WHILE loop.)

Yet, it is not only possible to solve many of these row positioning problems within the conventional boundaries of SQL by using self-joins, but by appropriately combining them with characteristic functions, solve these problems at a cost of just a *single* SQL statement employing a *single— two-way—* self-join.

In this article we show such solutions to the median and sequence splitting problems mentioned above, as well as to the problem of *clipping*, where one removes from a sorted data sequence a prefix and a suffix of some predetermined sizes. We also show novel solutions to the problems of computing *running* (or *cumulative*) and *sliding* aggregates over data sequences.

We also note up front, that any technique using self-joins over large tables immediately raises concerns over run-time efficiency. As it turns out, however, in many commonly arising cases— specifically, those involving table partitioning— the solutions presented are actually not inefficient, even when applied to large tables. However, efficiency issues are addressed only tangentially in this article, and will be covered more fully elsewhere. Our primary goal in presenting our solutions here is to illustrate their conceptual elegance, their compactness, and the interesting synergistic effect of using self-joins in conjunction with characteristic functions.

2 Finding a median

The problem of finding a "loop-free" SQL solution to a median problem has long been viewed as a challenge by SQL programmers, and has recently been posed as such and solved by Date [1,2]. In this section we present several much more compact and efficient, single SQL statement solutions for this problem. The first of these is presented in Figure 1 below, where we assume that data is presented in table **data(val)**, where **val** is non-NULL and numeric, and which contains no duplicates.

```
SELECT x.val
FROM data x, data y
GROUP BY x.val
HAVING SUM(δ[y.val<=x.val]) = (COUNT(*)+1)/2
```

Figure 1: *A single SQL statement solution to finding a median value.*

This solution employs a *self-join* (here, really a Cartesian product of table **data** with itself) and also relies on the use of the *characteristic function* technique introduced in [6,7] and then fully described in [8]. Expression δ[y.val<=x.val] denotes a characteristic function, which returns 1 if condition **y.val<=x.val** is True, and returns 0 otherwise. Readers unfamiliar or uncomfortable with this delta notation should replace expression δ[y.val<=x.val] as follows [8].

$$\delta[y.val<=x.val] = sign(1-sign(y.val-x.val))$$

Expression **SUM(δ[y.val<=x.val])** then, in effect, counts for a given x-value, how many y-values are less than or equal to that x-value. The HAVING clause then chooses precisely that x-value where this count is equal to half of the number of elements. (We rely here on Sybase-specific feature that the division of two integers returns (truncated) integer result.)

Note that this particular solution supports the *statistical* definition of median, where the median of a set must be one of the values in it. Indeed, given an odd number of values, this solution will choose precisely the middle one; given an even number of values, it will choose the *smaller* of the middle two. It is also possible to modify this solution to make it choose the *larger* of the middle two values, as shown in Figure 2 below.

```
SELECT x.val
FROM data x, data y
GROUP BY x.val
HAVING SUM(δ[y.val<=x.val]) = COUNT(*)/2+1
```

Figure 2: *Another solution to the statistical median problem: choosing the larger of the two middle values for even counts.*

Also note that it is possible to modify this solution to support an alternate *financial* definition of median, where in case of an even number of values, the median is defined to be the *arithmetic average* of the middle two. Specifically, consider modifying solution of Figure 1 as shown in Figure 3.

```
SELECT isnull(1.0*x.val/(COUNT(*)%2),
              (x.val+MIN(y.val/δ[y.val>x.val]))/2.0)
FROM data x, data y
GROUP BY x.val
HAVING SUM(δ[y.val<=x.val]) = (COUNT(*)+1)/2
```

Figure 3: *A single SQL statement solution to finding a financial median.*

If table **data** contains odd number of values, then expression **COUNT(*)%2** returns 1— operator % indicates *modulo division*— the SELECT clause expression becomes

```
SELECT isnull(1.0*x.val/1, ...)
```

and returns **x.val**, just as in the solution of Figure 1. (Built-in function **isnull()** returns its first argument if it is not NULL, and returns its second argument otherwise.)

If it contains even number of values, then **COUNT(*)%2** returns 0, and the first argument of the **isnull()** function returns NULL— we rely here on Sybase-specific feature that division by zero returns NULL. The control then transfers to its second argument, which functions as follows.

First, it selects **x.val**, which just as in the solution of Figure 1, is the *smaller* of the two middle values. Then it selects the smallest y-value larger than **x.val**, which is of course precisely the *larger* of the two middle values. (Here, expression **y.val/δ[y.val>x.val]** evaluates to NULL for all **y.val<=x.val**, and leaves those **y.val>x.val** untouched; the MIN aggregate, which of course ignores NULLs, then returns the smallest **y.val** larger then **x.val**.) Finally, it takes the arithmetic average of these two values, and returns it as the final result. (The use of 1.0 in the numerator of the first argument to the **isnull()** function is necessary to prevent truncation of this arithmetic average in case of integer values.)

Again, readers unfamiliar with the δ–notation should replace expression δ[**y.val>x.val**] as follows [8].

$$\delta[y.val>x.val] = 1-sign(1-sign(y.val-x.val))$$

Another important variation of this problem is finding medians in the presence of duplicate values. Assuming a table **data1(val, attr)** where **val** and **attr** are non-NULL and numeric, and which contains no duplicate rows, one solution to finding a median value is shown in Figure 4 below.

```
SELECT x.val
FROM data1 x, data1 y
GROUP BY x.val, x.attr
HAVING SUM(δ[(y.val<x.val) OR
                ((y.val=x.val) AND (y.attr<=x.attr))]) =
                                    (COUNT(*)+1)/2
```

Figure 4: Finding medians in the presence of duplicate values.

The basic idea behind this code, which is of course a modification of the solution of Figure 1, and as such finds a statistical median, is that attribute **attr** is used to "order" duplicate **val** values. Note that Boolean connectives AND and OR used in this solution are "virtual" in that no Boolean operations are actually performed. Instead, the above δ–expression is expanded as the following arithmetic expression [8].

$$\delta[(y.val<x.val) \ OR \ ((y.val=x.val) \ AND \ (y.attr<=x.attr))] =$$

$$sign(1-sign(1+sign(y.val-x.val))+$$
$$(1-abs(sign(y.val-x.val)))*sign(1-sign(y.attr-x.attr)))$$

Naturally, this solution can trivially be extended to any number of attributes, as long as they cover the key to the table.

Notably, none of the solutions presented above require the doubling of the data table as was done in [2], nor do they require the use of SQL-92 constructs. Furthermore, all of these solutions employ a *single* SQL statement *without subqueries* and use just two copies of the data table, instead of 3 statements with 4 subqueries, together effectively using 8 copies of the data table [2]. Note, however, that all of the above solutions rely on the data table containing no *duplicate rows*— a restriction also implicitly present in the solution of [2]. (As was illustrated in Figure 4, duplicate values themselves present no problems for our approach.)

Space limitations prevent us from considering many other interesting variations of this problem— e.g., finding median for non-numeric values, or finding it in the presence of NULLs. These will be considered elsewhere. In this article, however, we do consider one very important variation— namely, where the table needs to be partitioned by some attribute (or attributes) and the medians need to be computed for each partition.

Assuming now a table **data2(partition_id, val)**, where **val** is numeric, and which again contains no duplicate rows or NULLs, the SQL statement which computes the statistical median value for each partition is presented in Figure 5 below.

SELECT x.partition_id, x.val
FROM data2 x, data2 y
WHERE (x.partition_id = y.partition_id)
GROUP BY x.partition_id, x.val
HAVING SUM(δ[y.val<=x.val]) = (COUNT(*)+1)/2

Figure 5: *Computing median values for each partition.*

Except for the self-join on **partition_id**, and the use of **partition_id** attribute in the GROUP BY and SELECT clauses, this solution is the same as in Figure 1. Similar partition-based variations exist for solutions of Figures 2 through 4 as well.

In concluding this section, we note that solutions of Figures 1 through 4 rely on Cartesian products, and as such are inherently inefficient. (Due to their compactness, however, they may still be preferable to the conventional, row-at-a-time oriented solutions for small tables.) Due to the presence of an equi-join, solution of Figure 5 is of course fundamentally more efficient. Furthermore, efficiency of this solution actually depends on how the data is distributed in table **data2**. Specifically, assuming clustering by **partition_id**, this solution is likely to be much more efficient for cases where we have many small partitions rather than several large ones. The reasons for this have to do with data cacheing behavior; further discussion of this issue is beyond the scope of this article.

3   Dividing an ordered sequence of values into several intervals

Consider a problem of dividing (splitting) an ordered sequence of values into K *equi-sized* intervals (subsequences). The conditions of the problem are as follows: these intervals should be of *largest possible size*; also, should the sequence not divide "evenly" into K intervals, an additional *tail* interval of a *smaller* size is allowed. What we want to retrieve are the values that define the *end-points* of these K intervals, the positions of these end-points in the original sequence, and perhaps even the values comprising one or several of these intervals themselves. Naturally, the solution can explicitly reference the number of intervals K; however, the same solution must work for sequences of any length.

As an example, dividing an ordered sequence of 17 values into $K=3$ equi-sized intervals, should give us 3 intervals of 5 values each, with the end-points in positions 5, 10 and 15, and the fourth tail interval comprised of the remaining 2 values. Dividing a sequence of 18 values into the same $K=3$ intervals, should give us 3 intervals of 6 elements each, with the end-points in positions 6, 12 and 18, and no (or, equivalently, an empty) tail.

A single SQL statement solution to this problem for $K=3$ equi-sized intervals is presented in Figure 6 below. (Here we again assume our table **data(val)** from the previous section.)

```
SELECT x.val
FROM data x, data y
GROUP BY x.val
HAVING SUM(convert(int,δ[y.val<=x.val])) % (COUNT(*)/3) = 0
```

Figure 6: *A single SQL statement solution for dividing an ordered sequence of values into K=3 equi-sized intervals.*

Note the structural similarity between this solution and the one of Figure 1 for finding the median value. (The **convert()** function turns the results of the δ–expressions into integers; this enables modulo division in case of non-integer values.) Given a sequence of 17 values, the HAVING clause evaluates to True precisely for elements in positions 5, 10 and 15. The three values retrieved by this query then define the end-points of the first 3 intervals. Similarly, given a sequence of 18 values, the HAVING clause evaluates to True precisely for elements in positions 6, 12 and 18.

Naturally, this solution can be changed to work for any number of intervals simply by substituting this number in place of 3 in the HAVING clause. Indeed, it even works for $K = 1$ intervals— here, expression **(COUNT(*)/1)** becomes **COUNT(*)**, and the HAVING clause evaluates to True just for a single, last (largest) element of the sequence. While not particularly useful, this result is still absolutely proper with respect to our problem statement.

It is interesting to note that, as the above argument shows, by its very formulation our problem of dividing a sequence into equi-sized intervals with a possible tail is *not* a generalization of the median problem, but rather a different one. Indeed, here we want the *largest possible* single interval; in computing a median, we want what in effect is the *smallest possible* single interval, so that tail is still not larger in size.

Naturally, our solution can also be extended to retrieve the positions of the interval end-point values as well. All that is needed is to rewrite the SELECT clause as follows.

SELECT x.val, SUM(δ[y.val<=x.val])

Finally, our requirement that the tail interval be smaller than the other intervals imposes a restriction on the use of this solution. This restriction, which relates the number of values to the number of intervals, is best described by the following inequality

$N\%K < N/K$

where N and K are the number of elements and number of intervals respectively, and operator '/' indicates *integer division*. For example, in dividing into 3 intervals, this restriction means that we need 3, 6, 7, or 9 or more values to be present. The issue here is actually not just in the code, where we get modulo division by 0 or 1 in the HAVING clause, but rather in the statement of the problem itself. Indeed, it is simply not possible to divide a sequence of, for example, 5 values into 3 equi-sized intervals, plus a possible tail of a smaller size, in accordance with our problem definition.

In SQL this restriction can be expressed by the following condition

COUNT(*)%3 < COUNT(*)/3

stated here for the case of $K = 3$. This condition can then be incorporated into some IF statement protecting the query, or added with an AND to the HAVING clause, causing the query to return the empty table as the answer should it be violated.

Just as in the case of medians, intervals need not be computed over the single sequence comprised of all values in the table, but rather over separate sequences— quite likely to be of different sizes— defined over table partitions. As an example, assuming again table **data2**(<u>**partition_id**</u>, <u>**val**</u>) from the previous section, Figure 7 below shows a solution to the following, hopefully interesting specialized question: For each table partition, find the values comprising the middle third (i.e., second of the three) interval.

```
SELECT x.partition_id, x.val
FROM data2 x, data2 y
WHERE (x.partition_id = y.partition_id)
GROUP BY x.partition_id, x.val
HAVING SUM(δ[y.val<=x.val]) BETWEEN
            COUNT(*)/3+1 AND (COUNT(*)/3)*2
```

Figure 7: *Values comprising the middle third of each partition.*

In concluding this section, we note our solution can easily be modified to retrieve any points at any fixed position in any interval— for example, we can easily retrieve the interval *start-points*. More interestingly, our solution can also be easily extended to select a median (!) value from each interval. We leave these problems as a puzzle to the interested reader.

4   Computing running and sliding aggregates

Consider a table **data3**(<u>**id**</u>, **val**), where **id** is a key, **val** is numeric, and which contains no NULLs. Consider also a request to compute some *running* (or *cumulative*) aggregate over **val**— e.g., for every row to compute a *sum* of values in it and all the *preceding* rows— i.e., rows with **id** less than or equal to its own. A single statement solution to this problem is presented in Figure 8 below.

```
SELECT x.val, SUM(y.val)
FROM data3 x, data3 y
WHERE (y.id <= x.id)
GROUP BY x.id, x.val
```

Figure 8: *Computing running sum.*

Naturally, other running aggregates can also be computed by appropriately replacing SUM in the SELECT clause of this query. For example, by rewriting SELECT clause as

SELECT x.val, AVG(y.val)

we get *running average*. By rewriting it as

SELECT x.val, COUNT(*)

we get *unique numbering of rows*— i.e., every value gets assigned a unique id from 1 on in increasing order of ids. (A form of this solution was also described in [3].)

While this self-join technique is interesting in and of itself, its application to unique numbering of rows enables us to solve another important practical problem of computing *sliding* aggregates. (Computing sliding aggregates is essential to any system which needs to "smooth" experimental data.) Specifically, consider a table **data4(seq_id, val)**, where **seq_id** is now a key forming *contiguous sequence of integers*— e.g., 1,2, etc., and **val** is numeric and non-NULL. (Such a table can easily be generated from table **data3** by the above technique.) Consider also a solution of Figure 9 below.

SELECT x.seq_id, AVG(y.val)
FROM data4 x, data4 y
WHERE (y.seq_id BETWEEN x.seq_id–8 AND x.seq_id)
GROUP BY x.seq_id

Figure 9: *Computing the sliding average of 9 values.*

This code computes for every row the average of its value and values in the 8 immediately preceding (by **seq_id**) rows. (First 8 rows present a special case here, of course.) It is of course trivial to shift the sliding interval. For example, by rewriting the WHERE clause as

WHERE (y.seq_id BETWEEN x.seq_id–4 AND x.seq_id+4)

we can compute the average of the value with 4 immediate neighbors on each side.

Note that the solution of Figure 9 relies on the *contiguity* of **seq_id** values, which in turn generally requires a preparatory SQL statement. However, some important special cases can be solved in a single statement without the need for prior numbering of rows— e.g., computing a sliding average involving just the *immediate predecessor* and/or *immediate successor* of a row. This solution relies on a newly developed technique for selecting rows based on some MIN/MAX criteria, and will be presented in a forthcoming article.

5 Clipping

Consider a problem of *clipping*— i.e., retrieving a set of values without some number of smallest and largest values in the set. This problem often comes up in the context of processing experimental or financial data where one needs to remove what in effect are outliers. Assuming that values are presented in our table **data(val)**, one solution to a simplest case of this problem, which suppresses just the smallest and the largest values, is presented in Figure 10 below.

```
SELECT x.val
FROM data x, data y
GROUP BY x.val
HAVING SUM(δ[y.val<=x.val]) > 1
    AND SUM(δ[y.val>=x.val]) > 1
```

Figure 10: *Clipping the smallest and the largest values.*

Here, given some **x.val**, the first sum in the HAVING clause counts the number of y-values less than or equal to **x.val**, the second sum counts the number of y-values greater than or equal to it, and the HAVING clause suppresses retrieval of the two x-values where these counts are equal to 1— namely the smallest and the largest x-values, respectively.

Notably, other forms of solutions for this simplest case of the clipping problem exist as well— for example, one can replace the HAVING clause by a more conventional formulation, as shown below.

HAVING x.val>MIN(y.val) AND x.val<MAX(y.val)

In fact, given the particular non-standard features of Transact SQL, one can solve this case even without the self-join (and also without the GROUP BY, but still with the HAVING clause).

The importance of the particular form of the solution of Figure 10, however, lies in the fact that it is trivially extendible to clipping *several* smallest and/or largest elements from the set, as shown by the next example.

Naturally, our solution can also be adapted to the partitioned table case as well. For example, using our table **data2(partition_id, val)**, Figure 11 shows the code for clipping the 3 smallest and the 5 largest elements from each partition's subsequence.

```
SELECT x.partition_id, x.val
FROM data2 x, data2 y
WHERE (x.partition_id = y.partition_id)
GROUP BY x.partition_id, x.val
HAVING SUM(δ[y.val<=x.val]) > 3
    AND SUM(δ[y.val>=x.val]) > 5
```

Figure 11: *Clipping the 3 smallest and the 5 largest values from each partition.*

Note that those partitions having less than 9 elements will of course be dropped from the final answer to this query.

6   Conclusion

In this article we showed compact, single SQL statement solutions to several so called *row positioning* problems, specifically covering selection of medians, splitting a sorted sequence into several equi-sized contiguous subsequences, and clipping various numbers of extreme values from a sequence. We also presented novel solutions to the problems of computing running and sliding aggregates over data sequences.

The basis for our solutions was the synergistic effect of combining *two-way self-joins* with *characteristic functions* [6,7,8]. These self-joins permitted creation of query formulations where each value from the "primary" copy of the table was positioned for comparison with the appropriate value subset from the "secondary" copy of the table. Characteristic functions, then, allowed us to formulate multiple, and generally incompatible with each other, positioning criteria using the same secondary table copy, thus removing the need for additional table copies, and thus minimizing the number of required joins.

Another important contribution of this article was to show that these row positioning problems can be solved within the boundaries of conventional SQL, without the need to extend the language with specifically targeted built-in facilities, as for example was done in the Red Brick system [4,5].

References

[1] C.J. Date. "Theory is Practical." *Database Programming and Design*, 5(9), September 1992.

[2] C.J. Date. "Shedding Some Light." *Database Programming and Design*, 6(2), February 1993.

[3] F. Pascal. "Will SQL Come to Order? (Part 1)" In *SQL Forum Journal*, 1(10), July-August 1992.

[4] "Relational Query Systems and Relational Database Management Systems." Red Brick Systems, Los Gatos, CA, March 1992.

[5] RISQL Language Specification. Red Brick Systems, Los Gatos, CA.

[6] D. Rozenshtein, A. Abramovich, E. Birger. "Single Statement SQL Solutions to the Table Pivoting and Folding Problems." In *SQL Forum Journal*, 1(12), November-December 1992.

[7] D. Rozenshtein, A. Abramovich, E. Birger. "Effective Implementation of Conditions as Expressions in SQL Queries." In *SQL Forum Journal*, 2(1), January-February 1993.

[8] D. Rozenshtein, A. Abramovich, E. Birger. "Encoding and Use of Characteristic Functions in SQL." In *SQL Forum Journal*, 2(2), March-April 1993.

A Novel Approach to Computing Extreme Values in Transact SQL

David Rozenshtein, Ph.D., Anatoly Abramovich, Ph.D., and Eugene Birger, Ph.D.

reprinted from SQL Forum Journal, Vol.2, No.5, September/October 1993

1   Introduction

In this article we look at Transact SQL solutions to two types of *extreme value* problems— so called *horizontal* and *vertical*. Horizontal extreme problems are concerned with selecting the *largest* or the *smallest* value from a vector of values comprising a row in a table. Conventional Sybase solutions to these problems require several Transact SQL statements, and thus several passes through the data, and are quite inefficient. We, on the other hand, have developed and present in this article a suite of single Transact SQL statement— and single pass through the data— solutions for them. These solutions are based, in part, on the *characteristic function* technique, first introduced by us in [2], and then further developed in [3,4,5].

Vertical extreme problems are concerned with computing the *maximum* or the *minimum* value in a column. While by itself this is a trivial problem for SQL, what interests us is the following related problem: Given some attribute, select other attribute values from the row or rows containing the extreme value (maximum or minimum) for that attribute. In this article we present a spectrum of solutions to this problem— from some very conventional to newly developed ones.

2   Computing horizontal extremes

In this section we present the solutions to several *horizontal extreme value* problems. We begin with the simplest case of selecting from two numeric values, extend the solution to handle NULLs, and then show how this selected extreme value can be used in the ORDER BY and GROUP BY clauses of a query. We then generalize our technique to select extremes from more than two values. We follow by considering extremes from among strings and datetime quantities. We conclude the section by considering an interesting application of our horizontal extreme technique.

Before proceeding, we note that there are dialects of SQL— e.g., of Oracle— which in fact provide *built-in functions* for computing the horizontal extreme values [1]. (In Oracle, they are **greatest(value1, value2, ...)** and **least(value1, value2, ...)**; these functions not only take variable number of parameters, but are defined for all data types, including strings, which in fact cause terrible problems in Sybase.) Given how frequently the need to compute these **greatest()** and **least()** expressions comes up in practice, we consider the absence of these functions as built-ins in Transact SQL to be a serious omission. Thus, techniques presented in this section are intended, in part, to compensate for this omission.

2.1   Retrieving the largest of two numeric values

Consider a table **scores(name, sat1, sat2)**, where **name** is key and **sat1** and **sat2** are numeric and non-NULL, representing students' last year's Scholastic Aptitude Test (SAT) scores for the two permitted SAT attempts. Consider also a request to compute the answer of the form **(name, bestSat)**, where for every **name**, the value of **bestSat** is the *largest* of the corresponding **sat1** and **sat2** values. (While this information is obviously relevant to this year's college admissions process, the fact that we are using "largest" here is just an example; all of the techniques presented below translate trivially to the "smallest" case as well.)

A conventional solution to this problem is presented in Figure 1 below. As one can easily see, this solution requires two passes through the **scores** table, as well as creation of the intermediate work table **temp(name, bestSat)**, two inserts into this table, and one pass through it to generate the final result.

```
INSERT temp
SELECT name, sat1
FROM scores
WHERE (sat1 > sat2)
```

```
INSERT temp
SELECT name, sat2
FROM scores
WHERE (sat1 <= sat2)

SELECT name, bestSat
FROM temp
```

Figure 1: *Conventional solution selecting for every* **name** *the largest of* **sat1** *and* **sat2**.

A much more efficient, single SQL statement, and very importantly *single pass through the* **data** *table*, solution is presented in Figure 2 below. A simple trace of this code easily verifies that the second expression in the SELECT clause does indeed implement the required "largest(sat1, sat2)" functionality.

```
SELECT name,
       bestSat = sat1 + (sat2–sat1)*sign(1–sign(sat1–sat2))
FROM scores
```

Figure 2: *A single SQL statement/single pass query selecting for every* **name** *the largest of* **sat1** *and* **sat2**.

What underlies this solution is a technique called *characteristic functions* [2,3,4,5]. The basic idea here is that expression **sign(1–sign(sat1–sat2))** acts as the characteristic function for condition **sat1<=sat2**, returning 1 if it is True, 0 if it is False, and NULL if one or both of **sat1** or **sat2** is NULL. (This last case will become relevant later.) This, in turn, allows us to effectively implement the "largest(sat1, sat2)" behavior using a simple, and legal in Transact SQL, arithmetic expression.

Because we will use this characteristic function expression quite often, for the remainder of this article we will use a shorthand notation $\delta[$**sat1<=sat2**$]$ for it. This notation

$$\delta[\text{sat1}<=\text{sat2}] = \text{sign}(1–\text{sign}(\text{sat1}–\text{sat2}))$$

is fully described in [4], which also introduces notations, as well as actual code expansions, for the other binary comparators: =, !=, <, etc., as well as for logical NOT, AND and OR.

Using this δ–notation, we can now symbolically rewrite our query of Figure 2 as shown in Figure 3 below.

```
SELECT name,
       bestSat = sat1 + (sat2–sat1)*δ[sat1<=sat2]
FROM scores
```

Figure 3: *A symbolic form for query of Figure 2.*

Given their improved clarity, we will use such symbolic query forms in most of the examples for the remainder of this article; the reader is reminded, however, that the δ–notation is just a shorthand, and has to be fully replaced by its legal equivalent in the actual Transact SQL code.

Consider now relaxing the restriction on table **scores** and allowing NULL values for **sat1** and **sat2**— a reasonable possibility, since some students take SAT only once. In this case, given a pair of SAT scores, one of which is NULL, we want to retrieve the other one for **bestSat**. If both of them are NULL, we want to retrieve NULL as the result.

A query that handles possible NULLs for **sat1** and **sat2** is presented in Figure 4 below.

```
SELECT name,
       bestSat = isnull(sat2/δ[sat1<=sat2], isnull(sat1,sat2))
FROM scores
```

Figure 4: *Handling possible NULL SAT values.*

Here, if neither of **sat1** or **sat2** are NULL, this query computes exactly the same answer as the one of Figure 2. Specifically, for non-NULL **sat1** and **sat2**, expression δ[sat1<=sat2] returns either 1 or 0. If sat1<=sat2, the first argument to the outer isnull() function becomes sat2/1, which is of course sat2, and which is then returned as the result. If sat1>sat2, on the other hand, then the first argument to the outer isnull() function becomes sat2/0, which in Sybase evaluates to NULL, and the outer isnull() function then returns sat1 as the result.

If, on the other hand, either or both of sat1 and sat2 are NULL, the δ-expression returns NULL, and the outer isnull() function transfers control to its second operand— the inner isnull() function, which operates as follows. For sat1 not NULL and sat2 NULL, it returns sat1; for sat1 NULL and sat2 not NULL, it returns sat2; for both sat1 and sat2 NULL, it returns NULL, exactly as desired.

In concluding this section, we note that in all of the above examples, arbitrary arithmetic expressions can be substituted for attributes sat1 and sat2. Furthermore, as we will show later in the article, expressions computing "largest(sat1, sat2)" may themselves be embedded in other expressions.

2.2   Sorting and grouping by the largest of two numeric values

Consider again our table scores(name, sat1, sat2) and a request to *sort* it by the largest of sat1 and sat2, descending. Conventionally, this problem can be solved in a manner similar to the solution of Figure 1, as shown in Figure 5 below. (For simplicity of presentation we are assuming no NULL values here; we also assume a differently structured intermediate work table temp2(name, sat1, sat2, bestSat).)

```
INSERT temp2
SELECT name, sat1, sat2, sat1
FROM scores
WHERE (sat1 > sat2)

INSERT temp2
SELECT name, sat1, sat2, sat2
FROM scores
WHERE (sat1 <= sat2)
```

```
SELECT name, sat1, sat2
FROM temp2
ORDER BY bestSat DESC
```

Figure 5: *Conventional solution to the sorting-by-the-largest problem.*

However, building on solutions of Figures 3 and 4, and using the fact that Transact SQL permits the use of expressions in the ORDER BY clause, we can define a single data pass solution to this problem as well. Specifically, Figure 6 below presents the solution for non-NULL SAT scores.

```
SELECT name, sat1, sat2
FROM scores
ORDER BY sat1 + (sat2–1sat1)*δ[sat1<=sat2] DESC
```

Figure 6: *A single pass solution to the sorting-by-the-largest problem.*

Figure 7 below presents a solution that handles NULL SAT scores as well. (In the presence of NULLs, solution of Figure 7 will place those students with both **sat1** and **sat2** NULL at the bottom of the sorted list.)

```
SELECT name, sat1, sat2
FROM scores
ORDER BY isnull(sat2/δ[sat1<=sat2], isnull(sat1,sat2)) DESC
```

Figure 7: *A NULL-handling single pass solution to the sorting-by-the-largest problem.*

As one can easily see, the difference here is just in which expression is used to implement our "largest(sat1, sat2)" functionality.

Another interesting problem is to *group* our **scores** table by the largest of the two scores, and then to compute for each group the number of rows in it. Our solution to this problem for the non-NULL case is shown in Figure 8 below. (The

NULL case is handled by appropriately replacing the expression implementing "largest(sat1,sat2)" in the SELECT and GROUP BY clauses.) Here, we again rely on Transact SQL's ability to group by expressions.

```
SELECT
        bestSat = sat1 + (sat2–1sat1)*δ[sat1<=sat2],
        COUNT(*)
FROM scores
GROUP BY sat1 + (sat2–1sat1)*δ[sat1<=sat2]
```

Figure 8: *A single pass solution to the grouping-by-the-largest problem.*

It is extremely significant that our "largest"-expressions are *just* expressions, and as such can be used anywhere where ordinary expressions can appear, including not only in the SELECT, ORDER BY and GROUP BY clauses shown above, but also in the WHERE clause and in the SET clause of the UPDATE command. Additionally, these expressions can also appear embedded in other expressions.

An important example of this capability is shown in Figure 9 below, which modifies solution of Figure 8, and counts students not by *individual* best SAT scores, but by 100 point *ranges* of SAT scores. (A related problem of efficiently computing histograms in SQL was also covered in [4].)

```
SELECT
        rangeOfBestSat =
                ((sat1 + (sat2–1sat1)*δ[sat1<=sat2])/100)*100,
        COUNT(*)
FROM scores
GROUP BY ((sat1 + (sat2–1sat1)*δ[sat1<=sat2])/100)*100
```

Figure 9: *Embedding "largest"-expressions in other expressions.*

Here, the '/' operator implements *integer division*; hence, division by 100 followed by multiplication by 100 in the SELECT clause is not a "noop," but in effect a "truncation" of SAT scores to the nearest hundred.

2.3 Extending the "largest"-expressions to more than two arguments.

The definitions of our "largest"-expressions extend naturally to more than two arguments. For example, for three non-NULL numeric **A, B** and **C**, the "largest"-expression is shown in Figure 10 below. (Note that this definition is "recursive," and can be trivially extended to any number of arguments.)

$$\text{largest}(A,B,C) = \text{largest}(A,B) + (C-\text{largest}(A,B))*\delta[\text{largest}(A,B)<=C]$$

Figure 10: *The "largest"-expression for three numeric arguments.*

2.4 *Finding horizontal extremes among strings*

As one can easily see, the essence of our solutions presented in the previous sections lies in the proper encoding of the "largest"-expressions. While numeric arguments present no problems in that regard, the situation is not nearly as good with the strings. The actual problem lies in the fact that there is currently no way of encoding in Transact SQL a single expression for $\delta[A<B]$ that would work for **A** and **B** of type char(n) or varchar(n) for all n.

We have discussed this problem in some detail in [4], where we also showed how expressions for $\delta[A<B]$ could actually be encoded for **A** and **B** of type char(n) for some specific, small n. These encodings, in turn, enable one to use for strings the solutions presented in the previous sections.

Our general solutions for the string case, however, are based on a fundamentally different approach. Specifically, assuming a table **data(name, A, B)**, where **name** is key and **A** and **B** are some attributes of type char(8) and non-NULL, consider the code of Figure 11 below. (Of course, this solution can be adapted to **A** and **B** of type char(n) for any length n, simply by replacing 8 with the value of n in the substring expression.)

```
SELECT name, MIN(substring(A+B, 1+8*num, 8))
FROM data, multiplier
GROUP BY name
```

Figure 11: *Retrieving the smallest of the two char(n) values.*

For the sake of variability, in this example we have chosen to retrieve the *smallest* of the two strings. Here, table **multiplier(num)** is an ancillary table containing exactly two single-value rows: 0 and 1. As a result of Cartesian product between the **data** and the **multiplier** tables, the query effectively considers every **(name, A, B)** row from **data** twice— first with **num=0** and then with **num=1**. The substring expression then evaluates to the A-value for the first time, and to the B-value for the second time. (The '+' operator indicates concatenation for strings.) The built-in aggregate MIN then selects the smallest of these two **A** and **B** values.

The technique underlying this solution was originally introduced in the context of a *table folding* problem described in [2]. Here, this technique allows us to in effect "trick" SQL, by using a vertical extreme function (MIN) to solve a horizontal extreme problem ("smallest").

The solution of Figure 11 can easily be extended to **A** and **B** being of different lengths— say char(6) and char(10), respectively. Indeed, all that has to be changed is the substring expression, as shown in Figure 12 below.

```
SELECT name, MIN(substring(A+B, 1+6*num, 6+4*num))
FROM data, multiplier
GROUP BY name
```

Figure 12: *Retrieving the smallest of two string values of different lengths.*

These solutions are also trivially generalized to select the smallest from among more than two strings. For example, finding the smallest from among three char(8) strings is handled by extending table **multiplier(num)** to contain three values: 0, 1 and 2; and changing the substring expression in query of Figure 11 as follows.

```
substring(A+B+C, 1+8*num, 8)
```

Note that this extension to more than two string arguments is quite a bit simpler from the programming point of view than for the case of numerics. However, it is also less efficient, since due to the Cartesian product involved, every **data** row will now be considered three time by the query. The case of three or more strings of different length is handled in a similar manner.

We leave it for the interested reader to work out the necessary modifications to the solutions of Figures 11 and 12 to appropriately handle NULLs.

In concluding this section, we note that because of Cartesian products and groupings involved, these solutions for strings are not as efficient as the ones dealing with numeric data. However, they still employ only a single SQL statement, which is advantageous in many situations— for example, one does not have to provide explicit transaction boundaries. Finally, we note that unfortunately the technique presented in this section does not extend naturally to the cases of sorting and grouping. (Although, it is of course trivial to add ORDER BY 2 clause to queries of Figures 11 and 12.)

2.5   *Finding horizontal extremes among datetime quantities*

There are in principle two approaches for computing horizontal extremes among datetime quantities. First, by using the built-in *date* functions provided by Sybase, it is possible to directly encode expressions necessary to use the techniques for numerics presented in the preceeding sections. (Indeed, in [4] we show the relevant definitions for all the requisite δ–expressions.)

Second, by converting datetime values to strings, we can use the techniques for strings, also already introduced. (In this case, one has to make sure that datetime values represented as strings retain appropriate sort order.)

2.6   Finding the attribute for which the extreme value appears

Our final problem in this section deals with one of many interesting applications of horizontal extremes technique. (Others will be considered in the forthcoming article.) Specifically, consider determining not the extreme value itself, but rather the attribute for which it appears. For example, given a table **compensation(name, overtime, bonus)**, which is assumed to contain no NULL values, consider request to compute the answer of the form **(name, bestPayType)**, where **bestPayType** is a *string* attribute with values "overtime" or "bonus", depending on which value is the larger one in that row.

Solution to this problem appears in Figure 13 below. (Note that the lengths of strings "overtime" and "bonus" are 8 and 5, respectively.)

```
SELECT name,
       bestPayType = substring("overtimebonus",
                     1+8*δ[overtime<=bonus],
                     8–3*δ[overtime<=bonus])
FROM compensation
```

Figure 13: *Computing the attribute corresponding to the largest of two values.*

Note the similarity of the substring expressions between this code and the one of Figure 12. (Compare the use of the δ–expressions here with the use of **num** in Figure 12.) This solution also extends naturally to more than two columns, as well as to using the column name computed in this manner in the ORDER BY and GROUP BY clauses. Again we leave the handling of the NULL overtime and bonus values to the interested reader.

3   Computing vertical extremes

In presenting solutions to the vertical extreme problem, we distinguish between two cases. In the first case, we want to retrieve *all rows* corresponding to some extreme value. For example, given a table **employee(name, age, ...)**, where **name** is key, we want to retrieve the names of *all* youngest employees— i.e., employees with the minimum age. In the second case, we want to retrieve *just one of the rows* corresponding to the extreme. Thus, in our employee case, we want to retrieve *some* youngest employee.

Note that, since SQL is fundamentally a set-oriented language, where the answer to any SQL query is formulated basically as "Select *all* rows from ... such that ...," the second case is a more interesting one. We will therefore essentially just gloss-over the solutions to the "Select *all* ..." questions and concentrate instead on the "Select *some* ..." variety.

Finally, due to space restrictions, we will ignore the issue of NULLs in this section, and leave it to the interested reader to determine which code modifications, if any, would be necessary.

3.1   Retrieving all rows corresponding to some vertical extreme

Given a table **employee**(<u>name</u>, **age**, **...**), Figure 14 below presents three conventional solutions to finding all names corresponding to the smallest **age**. (Again, we are using the "smallest" just as an example here; all of the techniques presented below translate trivially to the case of the "largest.")

```
(1) SELECT name
    FROM employee
    WHERE age = (SELECT MIN(age)
                 FROM employee)
```

```
(2) SELECT name
    FROM employee
    WHERE age NOT IN
              (SELECT x.age
               FROM employee x, employee y
               WHERE x.age > y.age)
```

```
(3) SELECT name
    FROM employee x
    WHERE NOT EXISTS
            (SELECT *
             FROM employee w
             WHERE x.age > w.age)
```

Figure 14: *Conventional solutions to finding names of all the youngest employees.*

An interesting Sybase-specific solution to this problem is also presented in Figure 15 below.

```
SELECT name, age
FROM employee
HAVING age=MIN(age)
```

Figure 15: *Relying on some Sybase-specific SQL extensions.*

This solution relies on Transact SQL's ability to include in the SELECT and HAVING clauses columns not mentioned in the GROUP BY clause, as well as to have a HAVING clause without a GROUP BY clause. For a detailed explanation of this extension the reader is referred to [6,7]).

All of the above solutions extend naturally to the case where the extreme value is computed not for the entire table, but rather for groups within the table. For example, consider changing our **employee** table to **employee2**(dept, name, **age, ...**), with **(dept, name)** being a key, and a request to compute the names of all youngest employees *in each department.*

Figure 16 below shows the appropriate modification to the first query of Figure 14. (Similar modifications can be made to the other two queries of Figure 14 as well.) Figure 17 shows the necessary changes to the code of Figure 15.

```
SELECT dept, name
FROM employee2 x
WHERE age = (SELECT MIN(age)
             FROM employee2 w
             WHERE x.dept = w.dept)
```

Figure 16: Conventional solution to extremes-within-groups problem.

```
SELECT dept, name, age
FROM employee2
GROUP BY dept
HAVING age = MIN(age)
```

Figure 17: Sybase-specific solution to extremes-within-groups problem.

3.2   Retrieving some single row corresponding to a vertical extreme

A problem of retrieving some *single row* matching the desired extreme is interesting because it in some sense contradicts the spirit of "conventional SQL." It is, however, solvable. Specifically, first consider solution of Figure 18 below, which uses a Sybase-specific **SET rowcount** feature, and accomplishes its task by *explicitly* limiting the output of the query to a single (first) row to be retrieved.

```
SET rowcount 1

SELECT name
FROM employee
ORDER BY age
```

Figure 18: Explicitly limiting query output to a single row.

Another solution, which uses a "concatenation" technique recently developed by us, is presented in Figure 19 below. (Here we reasonably assume that **age** values are non-negative integers with up to 3 digits, and that the type of **name** is char(12).)

    SELECT substring(MIN(str(age,3)+name),4,12)
    FROM employee

Figure 19: *Using a "concatenation" technique.*

What happens here is that we convert ages to strings, concatenate names to these converted ages, and then select the lexicographically (alphabetically) smallest of these concatenations. This selected row of course contains the smallest age— age values being at the "head" of the concatenations, and on its "tail" brings us the corresponding name. The **substring()** function simply extracts that name for the final answer.

Note that **str()** is a built-in Sybase function that converts integers into *right-justified* strings. This is precisely what we need, since the lexicographic ordering of such strings representing *non-negative* integers is the same as for the integers themselves. (This technique can also be used with fractional numbers, since **str()** also provides for precision.)

Also note that this query retrieves specifically the *lexicographically smallest* name corresponding to the youngest age. Finally, the smallest **age** value itself can also be retrieved, simply by including **MIN(age)** in the SELECT clause.

This type of solution of course works very well for strings themselves, and also extends naturally to any type of data which can be converted to strings *preserving the sort order*. (Interestingly, negative numbers alone can still be handled here by taking their absolutes, reversing the order in the aggregate, and then negating the result. However, handling combinations of negative and postive numbers, without something like uniformly increasing them all to be positive, does present an interesting challenge here.)

Also, there are situations where one can use the spirit of this solution, without actually converting values to strings. For example, consider a table **data(A, B)**, where **A** and **B** are both nonnegative integers, and **A** is of *known range*.

Specifically, assuming that **A**-values range from 0 to 99, the query in Figure 20 below retrieves the smallest **A** corresponding to the smallest **B**. (Operator '%' indicates *modulo division*.)

```
SELECT MIN(B*100+A)%100
FROM data
```

Figure 20: *"Concatenation" technique "without strings."*

We now consider a problem of finding some youngest employee in each department. Interestingly, solution of Figure 18 *cannot* be extended to accomplish this— **SET rowcount 1** command would limit the size of the answer for the entire query, not for each group. There is, however, a similar solution to this problem, based on the idea of *implicitly* limiting the number of rows, which uses a Sybase-specific notion of a UNIQUE INDEX WITH IGNORE_DUP_KEY, as shown in Figure 21 below.

```
CREATE TABLE result(dept char(12), name char(12))

CREATE UNIQUE INDEX result_ndx
        ON result (dept) WITH IGNORE_DUP_KEY

INSERT result
SELECT dept, name
FROM employee2
ORDER BY age

SELECT dept, name
FROM result
```

Figure 21: *Implicitly limiting output to a single row per department.*

Note that, even though on a first glance ordering should be done both by **dept** and **age**, ordering just by **age** is sufficient. Also, given that we are looking for the *smallest* age, should table **employee2** have a clustered index starting with **age** or **(dept, age)**, the ORDER BY clause can be omitted.

Solution of Figure 19, however, does extend naturally to "youngest by department" problem, as shown in Figure 22 below.

```
SELECT dept,
        substring(MIN(str(age,3)+name),4,12)
FROM employee2
GROUP BY dept
```

Figure 22: *Retrieving some youngest employee for each department.*

4 Combining horizontal and vertical extreme problems

In this section we look at an example problem that combines in it both horizontal and vertical extreme aspects. Specifically, consider a table **scores2(name, school, sat1, sat2)** which basically extends our **scores** table with the school of the student. Consider also a request to compute for each school the names and the **bestSat** scores of some "best" student and of some "worst" student. By "best" we mean here a student with the highest **bestSat** score; by "worst" a student with the lowest **bestSat** score.

Assuming SAT scores ranging up to 1600 (which means they must be converted to strings of length 4), **name** of type char(12), and no NULL values, a solution to this problem is presented in Figure 23 below.

```
SELECT school,
    bestStudent =
            substring(MAX(str(sat1+(sat2-sat1)*δ[sat1<=sat2],4)+name),5,12),
    bestStudentScore = MAX(sat1+(sat2-sat1)*δ[sat1<=sat2]),
    worstStudent =
            substring(MIN(str(sat1+(sat2-sat1)*δ[sat1<=sat2],4)+name),5,12),
    worstStudentScore = MIN(sat1+(sat2-sat1)*δ[sat1<=sat2]),
FROM scores2
GROUP BY school
```

Figure 23: *Combined horizontal/vertical extremes example.*

5 Conclusions

In this article we look at Transact SQL solutions to two types of *extreme value* problems: *horizontal* extremes concerned with selecting the *largest* or the *smallest* value from a vector of values comprising a row in a table, and *vertical* extremes concerned with selecting other attribute values from the row or rows containing the extreme value (maximum or minimum) for some attribute.

For the former, horizontal extreme problems, we have developed and present in this article a suite of solutions which implement the desired extremes as legal Transact SQL *expressions*. This in turn allows for very efficient, single Transact SQL statement, and single pass through the data, solutions which in effect compensate for the absence of the "largest(A, B, ...)" and "smallest(A, B, ...)" functions as Sybase built-ins.

For the latter, vertical extreme problems, we present a spectrum of solutions — from conventional ones involving subqueries and multiple data passes, to some newly developed, more compact and efficient solutions.

References

[1] Oracle SQL Language Reference Manual.

[2] D. Rozenshtein, A. Abramovich, E. Birger. "Single Statement SQL Solutions to the Table Pivoting and Folding Problems." In *SQL Forum Journal*, 1(12), November-December 1992.

[3] D. Rozenshtein, A. Abramovich, E. Birger. "Effective Implementation of Conditions as Expressions in SQL Queries." In *SQL Forum Journal*, 2(1), January-February 1993.

[4] D. Rozenshtein, A. Abramovich, E. Birger. "Encoding and Use of Characteristic Functions in SQL." In *SQL Forum Journal*, 2(2), March-April 1993.

[5] D. Rozenshtein, Y. Alexandrova, A. Abramovich, E. Birger. "The Power of Self-Joins: SQL Solutions to the Median and Other Row Positioning Problems." In *SQL Forum Journal*, 2(4), July-August 1993.

[6] Sybase SQL Server Commands Reference Manual.

[7] *Sybase Technical News*, 2(1), January 1993.

❖

Loop-Free SQL Solutions for Finding Continuous Regions in Data

David Rozenshtein, Ph.D., Anatoly Abramovich, Ph.D., and Eugene Birger, Ph.D.

reprinted from SQL Forum Journal, Vol.2, No.6 – Vol.3, No.1,
November/December 1993 – January/February 1994

1   Introduction

In this article, we explore different variations of the following basic problem. Consider some data table and two conditions over this table: the first condition imposing some *order* on rows within the table; and the second condition defining the notion of a *continuous region* in the table, where by continuous region we mean a *set of rows*, all of which satisfy this condition, and all of which are *adjacent to each other* with respect to our row order. What we want is to locate such regions in the data table, and retrieve or compute some information about them.

As an illustrative, and a very simple, example of this problem, consider a table **data(id, value)**, where **id** is a *key*. Let the first condition be that the rows are sorted (or clustered) by id. Let the second condition be that column **value** in these rows should be less than 5. Continuous regions are then defined to be sets of adjacent rows with **value < 5**. What we may want to retrieve are: all of the rows comprising each of these regions; or just the rows forming the boundaries of these regions; or some statistical measures of the values contained within the regions— e.g., means, standard deviations, etc.

Perhaps the most obvious application area for this type of problem is the analysis of time-series data. For example, consider a time-keyed series of stock trades. Having sorted the data by stock-id, and then timestamp, we may then want to find for each stock those periods where its price was, say, at or above a certain value; or, within a certain value range; or, was continuously rising (an obviously important phenomena); or, where each subsequent price was within some percentage difference of the previous price, thus giving the stock some measure of "price stability," etc. We may even want to impose some additional constrains— say, that this period has to be of some specific duration; or, that it must occur during certain time of day, etc.

As another example, consider a time-series of data reporting on the lengths of some queues, which could be as diverse as I/O queues in some computer system, or check-out register queues at a supermarket. We may be interested in those periods where the average queue length was above some threshold— so that one could plan for allocation of additional queue consuming resources during those time periods. Other types of applications exist as well.

The most natural, and probably most efficient, solutions to these types of problems are the ones based on *sequential processing* of data. Thus, perhaps the most straightforward approach to finding continuous regions is to write a 3GL program, which would sequentially process the rows as they are retrieved in an appropriate order from the database, and would then post results back to the database, if necessary. Such sequential processing can also be achieved wholly within Transact SQL— either by using a WHILE loop and a **SET rowcount 1** technique, or by using *cursors*, which are available as part of System 10 Sybase Release.

In this article, however, we look at "pure" SQL solutions to this problem— i.e., the ones which do not use explicit loops— either external or provided by Transact SQL, and also which can be posed as single Transact SQL statements. While these solutions would most probably lose out in an efficiency contest with the sequential-processing ones, they are still of substantial interest. First, because they showcase the expressive power of SQL; and, second, because they are extremely compact, quite easy to program (once understood), do not involve the use of other languages, and for small to medium table sizes, quite efficient.

2 A simple example of the continuous region problem

We begin with an elaboration on the example from the Introduction. Consider a table **data(id, value)**, where **id** is an *integer key* forming a *compact*— i.e., *contiguously numbered*— sequence. Assume that this table contains no NULLs, and visualize it as *sorted* (*clustered*) by ids. Consider also a request to retrieve ids of exactly those rows from this data table which form *continuous regions* of rows with **value = 0**— in other words, those rows with **value = 0** that have an *immediate* *neighbor* also with **value** = 0. A solution to this problem, which is essentially self-explanatory, is presented in Figure 1 below.

```
SELECT DISTINCT x.id
FROM data x, data y
WHERE (x.value = 0)
    AND (y.value = 0)
    AND ((y.id = x.id+1) OR (y.id = x.id−1))
```

Figure 1: *Retrieving ids of rows comprising continuous regions with* **value** = 0.

This basic problem and its solution can now be generalized along the following several orthogonal dimensions. First, one can impose other, more complex conditions on values. Second, one can impose constraints on the size of the regions. Third, one can relax the assumption that ids form a contiguous sequence of integers; indeed, one can even extend this problem to non-numeric ids. Finally, one can restate this problem somewhat, and request that only the region boundaries, rather than all of the rows comprising the regions, be retrieved.

As its turns out, in presenting these extensions, it is convenient to first consider all of the cases involving contiguous ids, and only then look at non-compact id sequences.

3   Imposing complex conditions on values

In imposing conditions on values, it is convenient to distinguish between two types of conditions: *absolute* and *relative*. Examples of absolute conditions, which are conditions based just on the value in the row itself, are for the values to be less than some constant (e.g., **value < 5**), or to be within some range (e.g., **value BETWEEN 0 AND 7**), or even to satisfy some computational criteria (e.g., assuming integer values, be *even*— **value%2 = 0**). Such conditions can trivially be incorporated into the query of Figure 1, simply by appropriately replacing expressions **(x.value = 0)** and **(y.value = 0)** in its WHERE clause.

Relative conditions are expressed in terms of a relationship between the value in the row and the values in its neighbors. A very important example of such conditions is the requirement that values *monotonically increase* within the region— in other words, that the sequence of values be ordered with respect to the '<=' operator. Assuming the same table **data(id, value)** with contiguous ids, a solution to this problem is presented in Figure 2 below. (Note that since **x.value**'s are no longer constant here, it makes sense to retrieve them as well.)

```
SELECT DISTINCT x.id, x.value
FROM data x, data y
WHERE (y.value >= x.value) AND (y.id = x.id+1)
    OR (y.value <= x.value) AND (y.id = x.id–1)
```

Figure 2: *Retrieving rows comprising the regions defined by monotonically increasing values.*

4   Constraining sizes of regions

Note that the very notion of continuous regions imposes an implicit requirement that these regions contain at least two rows. The problem of imposing other constraints on region sizes is actually quite complex. For example, consider extending the solution of Figure 1 by requiring that continuous regions with **value = 0** have at least eight rows. Assuming the same table **data**, a conventional solution to this problem is shown in Figure 3 below.

```
SELECT DISTINCT x.id
FROM data x, data y, data z
WHERE (y.id <= x.id)
    AND (x.id <= z.id)
    AND (z.id–y.id >= 7)
    AND NOT EXISTS (SELECT *
                    FROM data w
                    WHERE (y.id <= w.id)
                    AND (w.id <= z.id)
                    AND (w.value != 0))
```

Figure 3: *Retrieving continuous regions of at least 8 rows with **value** = 0.*

Here, the outer query considers all regions of eight rows or more bordered by rows **y** and **z**. (While in SQL symbols **y** and **z** stand for *table aliases*, in tracing the SQL code it is convenient, and indeed proper, to view them as *tuple*, or *row*, *variables*.) The subquery then ensures that these regions do not contain any values other than 0. The outer query then retrieves all those rows **x** which fall into such regions.

Note that the solution of Figure 3 uses four copies of the **data** table, and as such is quite inefficient. Another solution to this problem, which notably uses only two copies of the **data** table, is shown in Figure 4 below.

```
SELECT x.id
FROM data x, data y
GROUP BY x.id
HAVING
    (SUM(δ[x.id <= y.id <= x.id+7]) = 8)
        AND (SUM(abs(y.value)/δ[x.id <= y.id <= x.id+7]) = 0)
OR (SUM(δ[x.id–1 <= y.id <= x.id+6]) = 8)
        AND (SUM(abs(y.value)/δ[x.id-1 <= y.id <= x.id+6]) = 0)
OR (SUM(δ[x.id–2 <= y.id <= x.id+5]) = 8)
        AND (SUM(abs(y.value)/δ[x.id–2 <= y.id <= x.id+5]) = 0)
    ......
OR (SUM(δ[x.id–7 <= y.id <= x.id]) = 8)
        AND (SUM(abs(y.value)/δ[x.id–7 <= y.id <= x.id]) = 0)
```

Figure 4: *A solution for retrieving continuous regions of at least 8 rows with* **value = 0**, *which uses only two copies of the data table.*

For clarity, this query is shown in its symbolic, shorthand form, which uses the so called *delta* notation, denoted by Greek δ. This notation was introduced in [3] to stand for *characteristic function* expressions for logical conditions. Essentially, notation δ[...] returns 1 if its argument, which is some logical condition, evaluates to True; it returns 0 if its argument evaluates to False; and it returns NULL if its argument evaluates to NULL. (This latter case is not relevant to the present article.)

In order to run this query, all of the δ–notations have to be properly replaced by actual Transact SQL expressions. For example, the first two δ–notations are replaced as follows.

$$\delta[x.id <= y.id <= x.id+7] =$$
$$sign(1–sign(x.id-y.id))*sign(1–sign(y.id–x.id–7))$$

$$\delta[x.id–1 <= y.id <= x.id+6] =$$
$$sign(1–sign(x.id–1–y.id))*sign(1–sign(y.id–x.id–6))$$

Other replacements are done in the similar fashion. (For general rules on how to encode characteristic function expressions in Transact SQL, the reader is referred to [3].)

To understand how this query works, consider the first disjunct of the HAVING clause.

$$(SUM(\delta[x.id <= y.id <= x.id+7]) = 8)$$
$$AND (SUM(abs(y.value)/\delta[x.id <= y.id <= x.id+7]) = 0)$$

Here, we make an assumption that **x** is the first row in the region. The δ–expression $\delta[\mathbf{x.id <= y.id <= x.id+7}]$ returns 1 for the eight contiguous rows **y** starting at **x**, and returns 0 for all other rows. The effect of the first SUM is then to ensure that the region indeed consists of exactly eight rows.

Consider now the second SUM. Here every **y.value** is divided by our δ–expression. Since division by 0 returns NULL in Sybase, the effect of this division is that all **y.value**'s outside of our region of eight are turned into NULLs, while the eight **y.value**'s inside the region are left untouched. Since NULLs are ignored in the SUM aggregations, the second SUM effectively adds up just the eight values in the region. Equating the resulting sum to zero has the effect of checking that every one of them is 0. (The use of the built in absolute value function **abs()** ensures that positive and negative values do not cancel each other here.)

The other seven disjuncts in the HAVING clause work is a similar manner. (For the sake of brevity, we have not explicitly shown all of them in Figure 4.) For example, the second disjunct assumes that **x** is the second row in the region. The last disjunct assumes that it is the last, eighth row in the region.

Note that, even though this query sets up the region size to be *exactly* eight, the question posed is actually for regions of *at least* eight rows. (Longer regions will simply be found by multiple disjuncts.) Also note that this solution extends to other region sizes as well. Here, however, even though the query still uses only two copies of the data table, the number of disjuncts in its HAVING clause has to be explicitly changed to match the region size.

It turns out, however, that there is a much better solution to this problem, which not only uses just two copies of the data table, but which is *universally applicable to any region size.* This solution, formulated here for region size of at least eight rows, is shown in Figure 5 below.

```
SELECT x.id
FROM data x, data y
WHERE (x.value = 0)
GROUP BY x.id
HAVING
    isnull(MIN(y.id/(δ[y.id > x.id]*δ[y.value != 0])) – 1,
                        isnull(MAX(y.id/δ[y.id > x.id]), x.id))
  – isnull(MAX(y.id/(δ[y.id < x.id]*δ[y.value != 0])) + 1,
                        isnull(MIN(y.id/δ[y.id < x.id]), x.id))
  >= 7
```

Figure 5: *A universal, two-copy of the data table solution for retrieving continuous regions of at least eight rows with* **value = 0**.

As with Figure 4, this solution is shown in its symbolic form, which requires expansion of all δ–expressions in the actual code, as follows.

$$\delta[y.id > x.id] \quad = 1-\text{sign}(1-\text{sign}(y.id-x.id))$$
$$\delta[y.id < x.id] \quad = 1-\text{sign}(1+\text{sign}(y.id-x.id))$$
$$\delta[y.value != 0] = \text{abs}(\text{sign}(y.value))$$

To understand how this code works, consider first the following expression from the minuend in the HAVING clause.

$$MIN(y.id/(\delta[y.id > x.id]*\delta[y.value != 0])) - 1$$

The only **y.id**'s that "survive" division by the two δ–expressions are the ones from the rows which both (1) follow the x-row in the id sequence, and (2) have a non-zero value. (The rest of the **y.id**'s are turned into NULLs.) The MIN aggregate then computes the smallest id from these surviving rows, which is of course the id of the nearest, non-zero-valued row to the right of **x**. Subtracting 1 from that **y.id** gives us the right boundary of the region containing **x**.

Note, however, that there are two cases not accounted for in the above analysis. First, it may be that, while there are rows following **x**, all of them have **value = 0**. Second, **x** itself may be the last row— i.e., have the highest id, and thus there would be no rows following it.

In both of these cases, *all* **y.id**'s under MIN would be turned to NULLs, and the MIN itself would return NULL. In that case, the outer **isnull()** function of the minuend would shift the computation to its second argument

$$isnull(MAX(y.id/\delta[y.id > x.id]), x.id)$$

which functions as follows. First, if there actually are y-rows after **x**, then **y.id**'s for all of them would be preserved by the division, while the rest of the **y.id**'s would be turned to NULL. The MAX aggregate would then compute the largest **y.id**, which would of course be the id of the last row in the table. This **y.id** would then be returned as the final result, exactly as desired. If there are no rows after **x**, then all **y.id**'s would be turned to NULL, the MAX aggregate would return NULL, and the inner **isnull()** function would return **x.id** itself, again exactly as appropriate.

Thus, the minuend expression

$$isnull(MIN(y.id/(\delta[y.id > x.id]*\delta[y.value != 0])) - 1,$$
$$isnull(MAX(y.id/\delta[y.id > x.id]), x.id))$$

correctly computes the id of the last row in the region containing **x**. Similarly, the subtrahend expression

$$isnull(MAX(y.id/(\delta[y.id < x.id]*\delta[y.value != 0])) + 1,$$
$$isnull(MIN(y.id/\delta[y.id < x.id]), x.id))$$

computes the id of the first row in the region containing **x**. Requiring that the difference between the two be greater than or equal to 7 is the same as asking for the region to contain at least eight rows.

Note that unlike the code of Figure 4, the solution of Figure 5 trivially adapts to other region sizes, simply by modifying the value of constant 7 in its HAV-ING clause. (Also note that the HAVING clause of this query in effect simulates condition (**z.id-y.id >= 7**) in the WHERE clause of the query of Figure 3, but does so without the two extra copies of the data table.)

5 Combining conditions on values with constraints on region sizes

It turns out that it is quite easy to combine *absolute* conditions on values with constraints on region sizes. Consider again the query of Figure 5. Adding **x.value** to its SELECT and GROUP BY clauses, changing condition (**x.value = 0**) to (**x.value < 5**) in the WHERE clause, and replacing expressions δ[**y.value != 0**] to δ[**y.value >= 5**] in the HAVING clause, gives us a query which computes the regions of at least eight rows with **value < 5**. The expansion for expression δ[**y.value >= 5**] is shown below.

$$\delta[y.value >= 5] = sign(1+sign(y.value-5))$$

Efficiently combining relative conditions on values— such as their monotonicity— with constraints on region sizes is more complex and is not addressed in this article.

6 Retrieving boundaries of the regions

We now reformulate our original problem somewhat, to specifically retrieve region boundaries— i.e., the *first* and the *last* rows— rather then their content. The simplest example of this reformulation is as follows. Consider again our table data($\underline{id}$, **value**), where **id** sequence is still compact, and a request to compute the answer of the form (**startId, endId**), where a row **<s, e>** indicates that our data table contains continuous region of rows with **value = 0**, *starting* at row with **id = s** and *ending* at row with **id = e**. One solution to this problem is presented in Figure 6 below.

```
SELECT startId = x.id, endId = y.id
FROM data x, data y
WHERE (x.id < y.id)
    AND NOT EXISTS (SELECT *
                        FROM data z
(1)                     WHERE (x.id <= z.id) AND
                               (z.id <= y.id) AND
                               (z.value != 0)
(2)                     OR   (z.id = y.id+1) AND
                               (z.value = 0)
(3)                     OR   (z.id = x.id–1) AND
                               (z.value = 0))
```

Figure 6: *Retrieving boundaries of contiguous regions with* **value = 0**.

What this solution essentially does is the following. First, it considers every pair of *distinct* rows **x** and **y**, where **x** comes before **y** (condition **x.id < y.id** ensures this). Then it makes sure that (1) all rows between **x** and **y** *inclusive* have value 0; (2) if it exists, the row immediately following **y** has a non-zero value; (3) if it exists, the row immediately preceding **x** also has a non-zero value.

Note that we can combine this problem formulation with more complex conditions on values and with constraints on region sizes. Indeed, imposing the latter constraints is trivial, since the region size can be computed here quite simply as (**y.id–x.id+1**). (Thus, all that one needs to do is impose some suitable condition on this size in the WHERE clause of the outer query— e.g., (**y.id–x.id >= 7**) for region size of eight or more rows.)

Efficient imposition of absolute constraints on values is also trivial here, and is handled by suitably replacing conditions (**y.value != 0**) and (**y.value = 0**) in the subquery. Efficiently imposing relative conditions is again more complex and will be considered elsewhere.

Note that solution of Figure 6 requires three copies of the data table— two to fix the boundaries, and the third to act as a kind of a "shuttle" between them. There exists, however, a solution to this problem which only requires two copies of the data table. This solution, which is based on solution of Figure 5 is presented in Figure 7 below.

```
SELECT x.id,
    isnull(MIN(y.id/(δ[y.id > x.id]*δ[y.value != 0])) – 1,
                                MAX(y.id/δ[y.id > x.id]))
FROM data x, data y
WHERE (x.value = 0)
GROUP BY x.id
HAVING
        isnull(MIN(y.id/(δ[y.id > x.id]*δ[y.value != 0])) – 1,
            MAX(y.id/δ[y.id > x.id])) > x.id
    AND isnull(MAX(y.id/(δ[y.id < x.id]*δ[y.value != 0])) + 1,
            isnull(MIN(y.id/δ[y.id < x.id]), x.id)) = x.id
```

Figure 7: *A two-copy of the data table solution for retrieving boundaries of continuous regions, over compact ids.*

Here, expression **x.id** in the SELECT clause retrieves the id of the left boundary of the region— the second conjunct of the HAVING clause, which is copied verbatim from the subtrahend of Figure 5, ensures that. The second expression in the SELECT clause computes the id of the region's right boundary. This expression, which is also repeated in the first conjunct of the HAVING clause, is a small simplification of the minuend from Figure 5.

Interestingly, a variant of this problem was previously presented and solved in [1, 2]. As stated, and as adapted to our example, the problem was to retrieve "all the sets of n consecutive" rows with **value = 0**. Figure 8 below shows solution of [2], again adapted to our table **data** for region size of eight.

```
SELECT id, ' thru ', id+7
FROM data x
WHERE (value = 0)
    AND (0 = ALL (SELECT value
                  FROM data y
                  WHERE (x.id < y.id)
                    AND (y.id <= x.id+7)))
```

Figure 8: *Adaptation of solution of [2] to our example.*

Upon closer examination, however, it becomes clear that this solution does not actually solve the boundary problem in its strict sense, in that it does not retrieve *proper boundaries*. For example, given some ten-row region of zero-valued rows, numbered say 101 through 110, the query of Figure 8 would return the following three rows in its answer: **<101 thru 108>**, **<102 thru 109>**, and **<103 thru 110>**. Yet rows 102, 103, 108 and 109 are not boundaries in the strict sense of the term.

So, what this query actually attempts to solve is a form of the "region content" problem— specifically, it retrieves ids of the first rows of all continuous regions of eight rows with **value = 0**. (Note that only the first row is actually *retrieved* here; the id of the last row is simply *computed*. We will return to this point shortly.)

In addition, solution of Figure 8 suffers from the following limitations. First, it does not correctly compensate for the "table-end"-effects. In fact, it even generates misleading results. Specifically, consider a data table where the *last three rows* are **<120, 1>**, **<121, 0>**, and **<122, 0>**. The query of Figure 8 would incorrectly and misleadingly generate row **<121 thru 129>** in its answer, even though there are no eight zero-valued rows starting at row 121, and in fact row 129 *does not even exist*. (This problem has to do with the fact that the id of the right boundary is simply arithmetically calculated here from the id of the left boundary, rather than retrieved.)

Also, this solution relies on the **= ALL** construct which is not available under Release 4 versions of Sybase servers. Finally, it cannot be naturally extended to handle *range conditions* on values. (Conditions such as **value < 5** can be handled here by using **5 > ALL** construct.)

On the other hand, solutions of Figures 6 and 7 properly account for the "table-end"-effects; can be implemented under currently widely available versions of Sybase; and can be extended to any absolute condition on values. In addition, solution of Figure 6 explicitly retrieves, not computes, the id of the region's right boundary. Therefore, it is trivial to extend it to also retrieve other attributes from this row as well.

7   Dealing with non-contiguous ids

The rest of this article deals with extending previously considered problems to the case of non-contiguous ids. The first of these, which simply extends the solution of Figure 1, is presented in Figure 9 below.

```
SELECT DISTINCT x.id
FROM data x, data y
WHERE (x.value = 0)
   AND (y.value = 0)
   AND (x.id != y.id)
   AND 0 = (SELECT SUM(abs(z.value))
            FROM data z
            WHERE (x.id <= z.id) AND (z.id <= y.id)
               OR (y.id <= z.id) AND (z.id <= x.id))
```

Figure 9: *Extending solution of Figure 1 to non-contiguous ids.*

To understand how this code works, consider some row **x** with **x.value = 0**. Consider now some other row **y**, such that **y.value = 0** and **x.id < y.id**— i.e., **y** *follows* **x** in the data table. Then, row **x** is in the answer if either **y** immediately follows **x**; or, if all rows **z** between **x** and **y** also have **value = 0**. This is exactly what the subquery does with the first disjunct of its WHERE clause. Similarly— and this is the role of the second disjunct— for rows **y**, which *precede* **x** in the data table.

Note that this solution not only *does not* require contiguity of ids, but it does not even require them being numeric! Should the ids be numeric, however, we can make the WHERE clause of the subquery more efficient, by rewriting it in an equivalent manner as

$$(x.id-z.id)*(z.id-y.id) > 0$$

If we assume that ids are still integers, however, then this non-contiguous id problem can be solved by a query which uses only two copies of the data table, as presented in Figure 10 below. (This solution is again written in its symbolic form, and must be expanded in the actual Transact SQL code.)

```
SELECT x.id
FROM data x, data y
WHERE (x.value = 0)
GROUP BY x.id
HAVING (MIN(2*(y.id–x.id)/δ[y.id > x.id] + abs(sign(y.value))))%2 = 0)
    OR (MIN(2*(x.id–y.id)/δ[y.id < x.id] + abs(sign(y value))))%2 = 0)
```

Figure 10: A δ–expression based solution for non-contiguous, integer ids.

This solution is based on a technique introduced in [5]. Consider expression **(y.id–x.id)/δ[y.id > x.id]**. Given some row **x**, this expression returns the "distance" between **y.id** and **x.id** for all rows **y** that follow **x**, and returns NULL for **x** itself and for all rows **y** that precede it. Each of these surviving distances, which is a *positive integer*, is then "extended on the right" with 0 for those rows with **y.value = 0**, and with 1 for the other rows. (This extension is expressed arithmetically by multiplying the surviving **(y.id–x.id)** by 2 and adding the 0 or the 1.) The MIN aggregate then selects the smallest of these expressions, which of cause identifies that y-row which immediately follows **x**, if such **y** exists. The *modulo division* (%) then checks if that row has **value = 0** or not. Similarly, the second disjunct in the HAVING clause checks that the row immediately preceding **x**, if it exists, has **value = 0**.

Note that this solution properly handles the "table-end"-effects. Another interesting feature of this solution is that the two MIN aggregates, which give us the *immediate successor* and the *immediate predecessor* for **x**, are computed here over the *same copy* of the data table.

8 Combining conditions on values with non-contiguous ids

Extending solution of Figure 10 to complex absolute conditions on values is quite straightforward. For example, replacing expressions **abs(sign(y.value))** under the two MIN aggregates in the HAVING clause with expression for δ[**y.value >= 5**] would give us a query, which *without relying on contiguity of ids*, would select continuous regions of rows with **value < 5**. (Note that the argument of the δ–expression here is the inverse of our condition. Thus, this expression would turn all **y.value**'s less than 5 to 0, and all other **y.value**'s to 1, exactly as required.)

It is possible to impose relative conditions on values as well in this case. Consider the query in Figure 11 below.

```
SELECT x.id, x.value
FROM data x, data y
GROUP BY x.id, x.value
HAVING (MIN(2*(y.id–x.id)/δ[y.id > x.id] + δ[y.value < x.value])%2 = 0)
     OR (MIN(2*(x.id–y.id)/δ[y.id < x.id] + δ[x.value < y.value])%2 = 0)
```

Figure 11: Selecting regions with monotonically increasing values without contiguous ids.

In this query, expression **abs(sign(y.value))** under the first MIN aggregate from Figure 10 is replaced with δ[**y.value < x.value**], which again has the inverse effect of requiring that the **y.value** following **x** be greater than or equal to **x.value**. Similarly, the use of δ[**x.value < y.value**] under the second MIN aggregate has the overall effect of requiring that the **y.value** preceding **x** be less than or equal to **x.value**. Thus, this query selects continuous regions of rows with monotonically increasing values without relying on contiguity of ids.

9 Computing the region boundaries for non-contiguous ids

Computing the region boundaries is also possible here. Consider the solution of Figure 12 below. (Again all δ–expressions used here have to be fully expanded in the actual code.)

```
SELECT startId = x.id, endId = y.id
FROM data x, data y, data z
WHERE (x.id < y.id)
GROUP BY x.id, y.id
HAVING (SUM(abs(z.value)*δ[x.id <= z.id <= y.id]) = 0)
    AND (isnull(MIN(2*(z.id–y.id)/δ[z.id > y.id]
                         + abs(sign(z.value)))),1)%2 != 0)
    AND (isnull(MIN(2*(x.id–z.id)/δ[z.id < x.id]
                         + abs(sign(z.value)))),1)%2 != 0)
```

Figure 12: *Computing region boundaries over rows with **value** = 0 with non-contiguous integer ids.*

To understand how this query operates, observe the similarities between the constructs used here and the ones used in Figures 4 and 10. Specifically, given **x** and **y** as region boundaries, expression

$$(SUM(abs(z.value)*\delta[x.id <= z.id <= y.id]) = 0)$$

which is modelled after Figure 4, ensures that all rows in the region have **value** = 0.

The two expressions **MIN(...)** used above are also essentially borrowed, but now from Figure 10. The only difference is that now we want a row following our right boundary **y** to have **value** != 0, thus making **y** a "true" right boundary of the region. Similarly, for the row preceding the left boundary **x**.

The only other additions in this example, are the two uses of the **isnull()** function. The idea here is that if **y** is also the *last* row in the data table, then no **z** with **z.id > y.id** would exist, and the MIN aggregate would return NULL. Since this condition is actually OK in this case, the **isnull()** function would simply turn this NULL into 1, which would of course make this conjunct evaluate to True. Similarly for the case of **x** being the first row in the data table.

10 Combining all of the dimensions

In this section we look at one final example which shows how to compute region boundaries for non-contiguous ids in the presence of conditions on values and region sizes. Specifically, consider again our table **data(<u>id</u>, value)**, where **id** is an integer, although not necessarily compact, key and which contains no NULLs. Consider also a request to compute the answer of the form **(startId, startValue, endId, endValue, size, avgValue)**, where a row **<s, v, e, w, n, a>** indicates that our data table contains a continuous region of eight or more rows, whose *size* is **n**, and where **value < 5**, *starting* at row with **id = s** and **value = v** and *ending* at row with **id = e** and **value = w**, and where **a** is the *average* of values within the region.

Consider the query of Figure 13 below.

```
SELECT startId = x.id, startValue = x.value,
       endId = y.id, endValue = y.value,
       size = SUM(δ[x.id <= z.id <= y.id]),
       avgValue = AVG(z.value/δ[x.id <= z.id <= y.id])
FROM data x, data y, data z
WHERE (x.id < y.id)
GROUP BY x.id, x.value, y.id, y.value
HAVING (SUM(δ[x.id <= z.id <= y.id]) >= 8)
   AND (SUM(δ[z.value >= 5]*δ[x.id <= z.id <= y.id]) = 0)
   AND (isnull(MIN(2*(z.id–y.id)/δ[z.id > y.id] + δ[z.value >= 5]),1)%2 != 0)
   AND (isnull(MIN(2*(x.id–z.id)/δ[z.id < x.id] + δ[z.value >= 5]),1)%2 != 0)
```

Figure 13: Computing region boundaries over non-compact ids, with conditions on values and region sizes.

The only real additions here, as compared to code of Figure 12, are as follows. First, similarly to Figure 4, given region boundaries **x** and **y**, expression SUM(δ[**x.id** <= **z.id** <= **y.id**]) used in the SELECT and the HAVING clauses in effect *counts* how many rows fit into this region and thus determines its size. Second, expressions **abs(z.value)** and **abs(sign(z.value))** used in the HAVING clause in Figure 12 are replaced here by expression δ[**z.value** >= **5**]. This in turn ensures that, if it exists, the nearest row **z** following the right boundary **y** *does not* have **value** < **5**. Similarly, for the nearest row preceding left boundary **x**.

11   *Some concluding remarks*

In checking the code examples presented in this article, we discovered to our dismay that queries of Figures 3 and 9 do not execute correctly as written. To make the query of Figure 3 execute properly, we had to repeat condition

(y.id <= x.id) AND (x.id <= z.id) AND (z.id–y.id >= 7)

taken from the outer WHERE clause, in the inner WHERE clause as well. Since this is clearly an *equivalency-preserving transformation*— i.e., the transformed query means exactly the same thing, and thus should generate exactly the same result, as the original one— we consider Sybase's incorrect answer to the original query of Figure 3 to be a bug.

Similarly, in query of Figure 9, we had to replace condition

(x.id != y.id)

in the outer WHERE clause, by an obviously equivalent formulation

(abs(x.id–y.id) > 0)

and then again repeat the entire condition from the outer WHERE clause in the inner WHERE clause as well— the same type of bug as mentioned above.

Both of these problems were discovered in Version 4.9.2 of Sybase server running under VMS, and have been reported to Sybase.

Finally, on another topic, we note that in all of the examples considered in this article we simply assumed that the data was sorted by ids, thus in effect "trivializing" our first condition. However, this need not be so. The ordering condition can be quite complex, in that it can involve *several* attributes, of possibly *different data types*. Space limitations prevent us from considering such cases in this article. However, in [4] we show the techniques necessary for implementing such solutions.

References

[1] J. Celko. "SQL explorer: Models, Divisors, and Logic." In *DBMS: Client/Server Computing*, 6(8), July 1993.

[2] J. Celko. "SQL explorer: Home Alone." In *DBMS: Client/Server Computing*, 6(12), November 1993.

[3] D. Rozenshtein, A. Abramovich, E. Birger. "Encoding and Use of Characteristic Functions in SQL." In *SQL Forum Journal*, 2(2), March-April 1993.

[4] D. Rozenshtein, Y. Alexandrova, A. Abramovich, E. Birger. "The Power of Self-Joins: SQL Solutions to the Median and Other Row Positioning Problems." In *SQL Forum Journal*, 2(4), July-August 1993.

[5] D. Rozenshtein, A. Abramovich, E. Birger. "A Novel Approach to Computing Extreme Values in Transact SQL." In *SQL Forum Journal*, 2(5), September-October 1993.

❖

SQL Solutions to Computing the Median in the Presence of Duplicates

David Rozenshtein, Ph.D., Anatoly Abramovich, Ph.D., and Eugene Birger, Ph.D.

reprinted from SQL Forum Journal, Vol.3, No.2, March/February 1994

1 Introduction

In [3], we solved a problem of computing a median of a set of values comprising a column in a table with a single SQL statement using just a single, two-way join. We looked at a number of median problem formulations, including the so-called *statistical* as well as *financial* medians, and also considered computation of medians over table partitions. We presented solutions for the case of *no duplicate values*, as well as for the case *with duplicate values*, but no duplicate rows.

In this article, we extend and generalize solutions of [3] to tables actually containing duplicate rows. We begin by briefly revisiting solutions of [3] for two simple cases of median formulations over non-duplicated data. We then extend these solutions to tables containing duplicate rows, and discuss the intuition behind these extensions. We follow with the detailed arguments of their correctness, and conclude our presentation with an actual Transact SQL code segment corresponding to the most complex query considered in this article.

2 Computing statistical and financial medians among non-duplicated data

Consider a query of Figure 1 below, first described in [3]. Here, the data is presented in table **data(value)**, where **value** is non-NULL and numeric, and which contains no duplicates. (In this case, conditions of "no duplicate values" and "no duplicate rows" are, of course, equivalent to each other.)

SELECT x.value
FROM data x, data y
GROUP BY x.value
HAVING SUM(δ[y.value<=x.value]) = (COUNT(*)+1)/2

Figure 1: *A single SQL statement solution to finding a statistical median among non-duplicated values [3].*

This query is shown in its shorthand, symbolic form which uses *characteristic function* notation δ[**y.value<=x.value**], which returns 1 if condition **y.value<=x.value** is True, and returns 0 otherwise. In the actual SQL code, this δ–notation should be replaced by the following scalar expression [2].

δ[y.value<=x.value] = sign(1–sign(y.value–x.value))

To see how this query operates, observe that expression **SUM(δ[y.value<=x.value])** in effect counts, for a given **x.value**, how many **y.value**'s are less than or equal to it. The HAVING clause then chooses precisely that **x.value** where this count is equal to half of the number of elements. (We rely here on Sybase-specific feature that the division of two integers returns truncated integer result.)

Given an odd number of values, this solution chooses precisely the *middle* one; given an even number of values, it chooses the *smaller* of the middle two values, or as we call it the *left median*. Thus, this particular solution supports the *statistical* definition of median, where the median of a set is one of the values in it. (It is very simple to modify this solution to make it choose the *larger* of the middle two values, or as we call it the *right median*, as shown in [3].)

Figure 2 below shows a modification of this solution to compute an alternative, *financial* definition of median, also first presented in [3], which in case of the even number of values returns the *arithmetic average* of the middle two.

SELECT isnull(1.0*x.value/(COUNT(*)%2),
                              (x.value+MIN(y.value/δ[y.value>x.value]))/2.0)
FROM data x, data y
GROUP BY x.value
HAVING SUM(δ[y.value<=x.value]) = (COUNT(*)+1)/2

Figure 2: *A single SQL statement solution to finding a financial median among non-duplicated values [2].*

In addition to the previously discussed δ–notation, this query uses notation δ[**y.value>x.value**], which also must be expanded in the actual SQL code as follows [3].

δ[y.value>x.value] = 1–sign(1–sign(y.value–x.value))

Consider now the SELECT clause of this query. If table **data** contains odd number of values, then expression **COUNT(*)%2**, where operator '%' indicates *modulo division*, returns 1; the **isnull()**–expression becomes **isnull(1.0*x.value/1, ...)** and returns **x.value**, just as in the solution of Figure 1. (Built-in function **isnull()** returns its first argument if it is not NULL, and returns its second argument otherwise.)

If it contains even number of values, then **COUNT(*)%2** returns 0, and the first argument of the **isnull()** function returns NULL— we rely here on Sybase-specific feature that division by zero returns NULL. The computation then transfers to its second argument, which functions as follows.

First, it selects **x.value**, which just as in the solution of Figure 1, is the *left median*. Then it selects the smallest **y.value** greater than **x.value**, which is of course precisely the *right median*. (Here, expression **y.value/δ[y.value>x.value]** evaluates to NULL for all **y.value<=x.value**, and leaves those **y.value>x.value** untouched; the MIN aggregate, which of course ignores NULLs, then returns the smallest **y.value** greater then **x.value**.) Finally, it takes the arithmetic average of these two median values, and returns it as the final result. (The use of 2.0 in the denominator here is necessary to force regular, rather than integer, division in computing of the arithmetic average in case of integer values; because the **isnull()**

function forces the type of its first argument onto the second, the use of 1.0 in the numerator of the first argument is again necessary to prevent truncation of this arithmetic average in case of integers.)

3   Computing statistical and financial medians in the presence of duplicates

Solution of Figure 1 does not work correctly in the presence of duplicate values. The essence of the problem lies in the fact (and this is a key point here!) that SQL *cannot* distinguish between multiple copies of a value in its GROUP BY clause. (This is also the reason why solution of [1] does not work correctly in the presence of duplicates.) Thus, if some particular **x.value=v** is duplicated among the data, the Cartesian product taken by the query "repeats" the content of the entire table for each copy of **v**, and then all of these repetitions combine into the *same single group* associated with **x.value=v**. That, in turn, changes what is returned by the **SUM(...)** and **COUNT(*)** expressions in the HAVING clause, effectively *multiplying* their results by the number of copies of **v**. The HAVING clause of the query of Figure 1 then no longer properly describes the condition on the position of median, and causes the query to operate incorrectly.

For example, in case of the data sequence

1, 2, 2, 3, 4

none (!) of the data values is selected as the median by the query of Figure 1. Specifically, consider value 2, which is what should be selected as the median for this sequence. Because it appears twice in the data, the group associated with **x.value=2** becomes {1, 2, 2, 3, 4, 1, 2, 2, 3, 4}. Since there are now 6 elements with **y.value<=2,** the **SUM(...)** for this group returns 6; the **(COUNT(*)+1)/2** for this group returns (10+1)/2=5 (note that '/' symbolizes *integer division* here!); the equality fails, and the HAVING clause returns False. Since the HAVING clause fails for other **x.value**'s as well, the query incorrectly returns the *empty answer* in this case.

Solution of Figure 3 below, however, which is a modification of the one of Figure 1, does work correctly in the presence of duplicates.

```
SELECT x.value
FROM data x, data y
GROUP BY x.value
HAVING (SUM(δ[y.value<=x.value]) >= (COUNT(*)+1)/2)
     AND (SUM(δ[y.value>=x.value]) >= COUNT(*)/2+1)
```

Figure 3: *A single SQL statement solution to finding a statistical median value, even in the presence of duplicates.*

This query is again written using symbolic δ–notations, which must be completely expanded in the actual code. (Expansion of the second δ–notation is trivially similar to the expansion of the first, shown in previous section.)

Here, for **x.value=2**, the HAVING clause becomes

(6 >= 5) AND (8 >= 6)

which is of course True, and value 2 is thus selected as the median. (Note that there are 8 elements with **y.value>=2** in the **x.value=2** group.)

Notably, the HAVING clause evaluates to False for all other groups. For example, for **x.value=1**, it becomes

(1 >= 3) AND (5 >= 3)

which is False; for **x.value=3**, it becomes

(4 >= 3) AND (2 >= 3)

which is again False, etc.

While the detailed discussion of the correctness of this query will be presented later in this article, the basic arguments are as follows.

Consider some ordered sequence of n elements: e[1], e[2], ..., e[n], where n=2k–1 (i.e., n is *odd*) or n=2k (i.e., n is *even*). Consider also some value **v** from this sequence. If this value is duplicated several, say p, times in the sequence, then it will occupy *adjacent* positions e[i] through e[i+p–1], for some i. If it is unique, then p=1, and it will simply occupy a single position e[i].

Since, by definition, a (left) statistical median of this sequence is element e[k], then for our value **v** to also be a median value, it must be that e[k]=**v**. That, in turn, is equivalent to the following requirement.

(1)   i <= k <= i+p–1

Note that one way of reading the above formula is as follows. For a value **v** to be the median, its *leftmost copy* (which has index i) must be at or *to the left of* the median position k, and its *rightmost copy* (which has index i+p–1) must be at or *to the right* of the median position k. In other words, the sequence e[i] through e[i+p–1] of copies of **v** must "cover" the median element e[k].

As we will show in the next section, the HAVING clause of the query of Figure 3 evaluates to True precisely for that value **v** which satisfies formula (1) above.

The query correctly computing a *financial* median even in the presence of duplicates is presented in Figure 4 below.

```
SELECT isnull(1.0*x.value/sign(
              δ[SUM(δ[y.value<=x.value]) > (COUNT(*)+1)/2] +
              COUNT(*)%2
                                ),
        (x.value + MIN(y.value/δ[y.value>x.value]))/2.0)
FROM data x, data y
GROUP BY x.value
HAVING (SUM(δ[y.value<=x.value]) >= (COUNT(*)+1)/2)
    AND (SUM(δ[y.value>=x.value]) >= COUNT(*)/2+1)
```

Figure 4: A single SQL statement solution to finding a financial median value, even in the presence of duplicates.

In addition to previously discussed δ–notations, this query also uses notation

$$\delta[SUM(\delta[y.value<=x.value]) > (COUNT(*)+1)/2]$$

which must be expanded in actual code as follows [2].

$$\delta[SUM(\delta[y.value<=x.value]) > (COUNT(*)+1)/2] =$$
$$1-sign(1-sign(SUM(\delta[y.value<=x.value]) - (COUNT(*)+1)/2))$$

A completely expanded Transact SQL version of this query is presented later in this article.

The difference between this query and the one of Figure 3 is of course in the SELECT clause, and corresponds to the difference between the queries of Figures 1 and 2, except that the denominator under the **1.0*x.value** expression here is more complex.

The basic idea here is that, since duplication is now possible, the arithmetic average needs to be taken only in those cases where the number of elements is even *and* the two middle elements have *different values*. As we will show in the next section, the denominator under the **1.0*x.value** evaluates to 0 precisely in such cases. As we will also show, this is specifically facilitated by the use of the *strictly greater than* operator '>' rather than *greater than or equal to* operator '>=' in

$$\delta[SUM(\delta[y.value<=x.value]) > (COUNT(*)+1)/2]$$

The **isnull()** function then transfers computation to its second argument, which in turn returns the arithmetic average of the left and right median elements as the final result.

In all other cases, the denominator evaluates to 1, and the query properly returns the left median element **x.value** itself as the answer.

4 Correctness of the solutions

In this section, we present detailed arguments of the correctness of the solutions of Figures 3 and 4.

Assertion 1:

Query of Figure 3 correctly computes a statistical median, even in the presence of duplicate values.

Proof:

By arguments presented in the previous section, what we actually have to prove here is that, given an ordered sequence of elements e[1], e[2], ..., e[n], where n=2k or n=2k–1, a value **v** occupying positions e[i] though e[i+p–1] is retrieved exactly when formula (1), repeated below, is True.

$$(1) \qquad i <= k <= i+p-1$$

Given a value **v** occupying positions e[i] through e[i+p–1], aggregates for the group corresponding to **x.value=v** return the following results. (This is the multiplicative effect mentioned in the previous section.)

$$SUM(\delta[y.value<=x.value]) = p*(i+p-1)$$

$$SUM(\delta[y.value>=x.value]) = p*(n-i+1)$$

$$COUNT(*) \qquad\qquad = p*n$$

This, in turn, allows us to rewrite the two inequalities from the HAVING clause as formulas (2) and (3) below. (To avoid any possible confusion, we use the DIV operator to specifically indicate that we mean *integer division* here.)

$$(2) \qquad p*(i+p-1) >= (p*n+1) \text{ DIV } 2$$

$$(3) \qquad p*(n-i+1) >= (p*n \text{ DIV } 2)+1$$

We now look at how these formulas transform, depending on whether n and p are odd or even. (As it turns out, there are three cases: odd n/even p; odd n/odd p; and even n/any p. Since the last case is the simplest, we cover it first.)

Case 1: even n:

Assume that n is even (n=2k). Then, due to the *integer division* involved, expression (p*n+1) DIV 2 becomes equivalent to p*n/2, where '/' now means *regular division*, and inequalities (2) and (3) become

```
p*(i+p–1)        >= p*2k/2
p*(2k–i+1)       >= p*2k/2+1
```

Dividing both sides by p, simplifying the right sides, and rearranging the second expression, we get

```
i+p–1            >= k
i                <= k+1–(1/p)
```

which, by i, p, and k being *positive integers*, are equivalent to

```
i+p–1            >= k
i                <= k
```

which is, of course, the same as formula (1).

Case 2: odd n, even p:

Assume now that n is odd (n=2k–1) and p is even. Since p is even, expression (p*n+1) DIV 2 again becomes equivalent to p*n/2, and the inequalities become

```
p*(i+p–1)        >= p*(2k–1)/2
p*(2k–1–i+1)     >= p*(2k–1)/2+1
```

Dividing by p, simplifying and rearranging, we get

```
i+p–1            >= k–(1/2)
i                <= k+(1/2)–(1/p)
```

which, by i, p, and k being positive integers, and *p being even* (i.e., at least 2), are equivalent to

```
i+p–1          >= k
i              <= k
```

which again gives us formula (1).

Case 3: odd n, odd p:

Assume now that n is odd (n=2k–1) and p is odd as well. Since both n and p are odd, expression (p*n DIV 2)+1 becomes equivalent to (p*n+1)/2, and the inequalities become

```
p*(i+p–1)      >= (p*(2k–1)+1)/2
p*(2k–1–i+1)   >= (p*(2k–1)+1)/2
```

Dividing by p, simplifying and rearranging, we get

```
i+p–1          >= k–(1/2)+(1/2p)
i              <= k+(1/2)–(1/2p)
```

which, by i, p, and k being positive integers, are equivalent to

```
i+p–1          >= k
i              <= k
```

again giving formula (1).

Since all of the transformations applied in the three cases above were *equivalency-preserving*, we can thus conclude that formulas (2) and (3) taken together are equivalent to formula (1). Since formulas (2) and (3) represent the HAVING clause of the query of Figure 3, and since by arguments presented in the previous section formula (1) in effect defines the conditions of being a median value, we can further conclude that this query will retrieve exactly the median **x.value.**

In concluding this proof, we also note that all of the arguments made in Cases 1 and 3 above (Case 2 does not apply) hold if value **v** is not duplicated — i.e., p=1. Formula (1) simply becomes i <= k <= i

making e[i] a median exactly when it is situated in position k, just as appropriate. Thus, the no duplicates case is simply a proper special case in this argument. Q.E.D.

We now consider the query of Figure 4.

Assertion 2:

Query of Figure 4 correctly computes a financial median, even in the presence of duplicate values.

Proof:

Since this query has exactly the same HAVING clause as the query of Figure 3, by arguments presented in the previous proof, *only the median element* **x.value** would be chosen here for the SELECT clause. Thus, all that we need to show is that expressions used in this SELECT clause properly return this **x.value**, or its arithmetic average with the right median, should that be appropriate. To do this, we need to consider several cases.

We begin with the two cases of non-duplicated median.

Case 1: odd number of elements and no duplicates of median x.value:

In this case, expression **COUNT(*)%2** returns 1; the **sign()**–expression becomes **sign(δ[...] + 1)**, and since in the absence of NULL values all δ–notations evaluate either to 0 or 1, the **sign()**–expression returns 1 as the result. The **isnull()**–expression then becomes **isnull(1.0*x.value/1, ...)** and thus returns the median **x.value** as the final result.

Case 2: even number of elements and no duplicates of median x.value:

In this case, expression COUNT(*)%2 returns 0, and condition

$$SUM(\delta[y.value<=x.value]) > (COUNT(*)+1)/2$$

returns False. (This is because, as was argued in the comments to Figure 1, and also in more detail in [3], in case of *non-duplicated left median*, which is what is chosen by the HAVING clause for **x.value** in this case, the two sides of this expression are related by *equality!*)

The sign()–expression becomes $\text{sign}(\delta[\text{False}] + 0)$, and thus $\text{sign}(0 + 0)$, and thus returns 0. The isnull()–expression then becomes $\text{isnull}(1.0*\text{x.value}/0, ...)$, and since division by 0 returns NULL in Sybase, the computation transfers to the second argument of the isnull() function, namely to

$$(\text{x.value} + \text{MIN}(\text{y.value}/\delta[\text{y.value} > \text{x.value}]))/2.0$$

As argued in [3], the MIN expression then selects the *right median*, and the arithmetic average of these two median values is returned as the final result.

We now consider the two cases involving median duplication.

Case 3: odd number of elements with duplicates of median **x.value:**
Suppose now that **x.value** is duplicated several, say p, times. Consider condition

$$\text{SUM}(\delta[\text{y.value}<=\text{x.value}]) > (\text{COUNT}(*)+1)/2$$

where, since this is an SQL code segment, '/' indicates integer division. Substituting for the SUM and the COUNT, as was shown in the previous proof, we get

$$p*(i+p-1) > (p*n+1) \text{ DIV } 2$$

If p is even, this inequality is equivalent to

$$i+p-1 > k-(1/2)$$

If p is odd, it is equivalent to

$$i+p-1 > k-(1/2)+(1/2p)$$

Since i, p and k are positive integers *and there are duplicates* (i.e., p>1), *both* of these strict inequalities logically follow from formula (1) (i.e., i <= k <= i+p–1). Since **x.value** is median, formula (1) is True, and thus both of the strict inequalities above are also True. Thus, we can conclude that condition **SUM(...) > (COUNT(*)+1)/2** also evaluates to True.

The **sign()**–expression then becomes **sign(δ[True] + COUNT(*)%2)**, and thus **sign(1 + COUNT(*)%2)**, and since COUNT always evaluates to a non-negative number, the **sign()**–expression then returns 1 as the result. The **isnull()**–expression then again becomes **isnull(1.0*x.value/1, ...)** and thus again returns our median **x.value** as the final result.

Case 4: even number of elements with duplicates of median **x.value:**

Finally, suppose that **x.value** is again duplicated several, say p, times. Since the number of elements n is even, expression **COUNT(*)%2** evaluates to 0. Condition

$$\text{SUM}(\delta[\text{y.value<=x.value}]) > (\text{COUNT}(*)+1)/2$$

again becomes

$$p*(i+p{-}1) > (p*n+1) \text{ DIV } 2$$

which in case of even n=2k is equivalent to

$$i+p{-}1 > k.$$

What we know about the left median element in this case, however, is that

$$i+p{-}1 >= k.$$

So we must analyze two subcases: one for "equal" and the other for "strictly greater than".

Consider first the case where i+p–1 = k. The meaning of this equality is that the last, right-most copy of the median value is located *exactly* at position k— i.e., at the left median position. In other words, the right median position is occupied by some other value. In such a case, condition i+p–1 > k, and thus condition

$$\text{SUM}(\delta[\text{y.value}<=\text{x.value}]) > (\text{COUNT}(*)+1)/2$$

evaluate to False; the **sign()**–expression becomes **sign(δ[False] + 0)**, and thus **sign(0 + 0)**, and thus returns 0; the **isnull()** function transfers the computation to its second argument, and by the arguments of Case 2 above, the arithmetic average of the two median elements is returned as the final result.

Consider now the second subcase, where i+p–1 > k. The meaning here is that the last, right-most copy of the median value extends "over" the right median element as well— in other words, both median elements have the same value. In this case, condition

$$\text{SUM}(\delta[\text{y.value}<=\text{x.value}]) > (\text{COUNT}(*)+1)/2$$

evaluates to True; the **sign()**–expression becomes **sign(δ[True] + 0)**, and thus **sign(1 + 0)**, and thus returns 1, and the **isnull()** function becomes **isnull(x.value/1, ...)** and thus returns **x.value** as the final result, exactly as appropriate in this case.　　　　　　　　　　　　　　　　　　　Q.E.D.

In concluding this section, we note that expression **COUNT(*)%2** was included into the query of Figure 4 to handle precisely the case of the odd number of elements with non-duplicated median (Case 1 of the above proof). To put it another way, if this expression is removed, the query will return incorrect result exactly in this, and no other, case.

5　The actual Transact SQL code for computing a financial median in the presence of duplicates

Since the query of Figure 4 is actually quite complex, and in particular since it uses a nested form of δ–notations, in this section in Figure 5 below we present a fully expanded version of this query into Transact SQL.

```
SELECT isnull(1.0*x.value/sign(
                (1–sign(1–sign(
                    SUM(sign(1–sign(y.value–x.value)))+
                                            (COUNT(*)+1)/2
                    )))+COUNT(*)%2),
            (x.value+MIN(y.value/(1–sign(1–sign(y.value–x.value))))))/2.0)
    FROM data x, data y
    GROUP BY x.value
    HAVING (SUM(sign(1–sign(y.value–x.value))) >= (COUNT(*)+1)/2)
        AND (SUM(sign(1–sign(x.value–y.value))) >= COUNT(*)/2+1)
```

Figure 5: *Actual Transact SQL code corresponding to the single SQL statement solution to finding a financial median value, even in the presence of duplicates.*

6 Conclusion

In this article, we continue the development of a suite of single statement, loop-free Transact SQL solutions for computing a median of a set of values comprising a column in a table. In [3], which began this development, we presented solutions for a number of median problem formulations, including the so-called *statistical* as well as *financial* medians, and also considered computation of medians over table partitions.

All of the solutions of [3], however, assumed that the underlying data table contained no duplicate rows. Indeed, some of them were designed specifically for the case where the column in question contained no duplicate values; others did handle duplicate values, but relied on the existence of some known table key. In this article, on the other hand, we presented universal solutions for the median problem, which work in all cases, even if the table contains duplicate rows.

We began our presentation with a brief review of statistical and financial median solutions from [3] for the case of non-duplicated data, extended these solutions to handle tables with duplicate rows, and then discussed the intuition behind these extensions. We followed with the detailed explanation of the correctness of our universal solutions, and concluded with an actual Transact SQL code segment corresponding to our most complex query.

References

[1] C.J. Date. "Access path." Letters to the Editor. *Database Programming and Design*, 6(9), September 1993.

[2] D. Rozenshtein, A. Abramovich, E. Birger. "Encoding and Use of Characteristic Functions in SQL." In *SQL Forum Journal*, 2(2), March-April 1993.

[3] D. Rozenshtein, A. Abramovich, Y. Alexandrova, E. Birger. "The Power of Self-Joins: SQL Solutions to the Median and Other Row Positioning Problems." In *SQL Forum Journal*, 2(4), July-August 1993.
❖

Encoding Characteristic
Functions in SQL-92

David Rozenshtein, Ph.D.

reprinted from SQL Forum Journal, Vol. 5, Number 1, January/February 1996

1 Introduction

In [1,2,3,4,5,6,7,8], Rozenshtein, Abramovich and Birger describe a new relational programming methodology, called *linguistic optimization*, for writing compact and efficient SQL queries. The essence of this methodology lies in reformulating queries to require fewer passes through the underlying data tables than the conventional solutions.

For many types of important practical problems linguistic optimization methodology results in queries which are substantially — sometimes, an order of magnitude — more efficient than their conventional counterparts. These problems include: pivoting and folding tables [1], conditionally using attributes in the SELECT, WHERE, GROUP BY and HAVING clauses [2], computing histograms [3], computing medians [4,7], dividing data into sorted subsequences [4], removing outliers [4], computing row-wise minimums and maximums [5], attaching to column-wise minimums and maximums [5], and finding "continuous" regions of data satisfying some condition [6]. An introductory overview of this methodology is presented in [8].

To achieve the speed-up, linguistic optimization relies on a conceptual device called *characteristic functions*. The intent of characteristic functions is to "recognize" conditions. Syntactically, characteristic functions are expressed using the following "delta"-notation

$$\delta[\alpha]$$

where symbol α represents some condition (logical expression), and the notation $\delta[\alpha]$ is intended to return 1 if condition α evaluates to True, return 0 if α evaluates to False, and return NULL if α evaluates to Maybe (Unknown).

Structurally, characteristic functions are implemented (encoded) as scalar expressions, using the built-in scalar operators and functions provided by SQL. Since these built-in facilities differ widely among the various SQL dialects, so do the encoding schemes. Moreover, even within the same dialect, the differences in the built-in operators and functions for the different data types usually lead to a different encoding scheme for each data type.

With the advent of SQL-92, however, it has now become possible to develop a single characteristic function encoding scheme, universally applicable to all data types in all SQL-92 conformant systems. In this article, we show how this can be accomplished.

To motivate the discussion, we begin by presenting an example of a table pivoting problem, taken from [1], which represents perhaps the most common use of linguistic optimization in SQL. We then describe a system of characteristic function encodings for numeric arguments for generic Transact SQL [3], and present a solution to our problem using these encodings. We then show how characteristic functions can be encoded in SQL-92 using the CASE expressions, and recast our solution accordingly. We conclude the article with the discussion of several related issues.

2   A motivating example

Consider the following example of the table pivoting problem [1]. Let the initial data be presented in table **bonus(name, month, amount)**, where the **month** and **amount** values are numeric and non-NULL, and which contains for each person twelve bonus amount rows. (As conventional, we use attribute underlining to designate relational keys.) Let the desired result have the form **(name, janAmount, febAmount, ..., decAmount)**, which would contain for each person a *single row* with all twelve corresponding monthly bonus amounts.

As discussed in [1], conventional solutions to this problem require either twelve SQL statements, or a single SQL statement with a twelve-way join, each using twelve passes through table **bonus**, plus a very substantial additional computational overhead.

Consider, however, the solution of Figure 1 [8].

```
SELECT name,
    janAmount = SUM(amount*δ[month=1]),
    febAmount = SUM(amount*δ[month=2]),
    ...
    decAmount = SUM(amount*δ[month=12])
FROM bonus
GROUP BY name
```

Figure 1: *A symbolic form of the solution for the table pivoting problem.*

This solution is presented in a symbolic form, and should be viewed as a template for the actual SQL query that can be obtained from it by substituting proper scalar expressions for the twelve δ–notations.

To understand the intent of this query, however, consider notation **δ[month=1]**. Given a **month** value of 1, this notation returns 1. Given any other **month** value, it returns 0. (The NULL case is not considered here.)

Consider now the expression

janAmount = SUM(amount*δ[month=1])

ana consider the twelve data rows "belonging" to some person Smith. Of the twelve amounts from these data rows, only the January amount retains its original value, with the rest of them reduced to zero by the multiplication with **δ[month=1]**. Thus, the **janAmount** expression, in effect, simply returns the January amount for Smith, precisely as required.

The other eleven expressions for **febAmount**, etc. act in a similar way.

Note that this solution requires only a single SQL statement, and involves one pass through table **bonus**, plus the cost of computing aggregates, thus making this query fundamentally more efficient than the conventional ones.

3 Encoding characteristic functions in generic Transact SQL

Since characteristic functions are implemented (encoded) as *scalar expressions*, they have to be expressed using the built-in scalar operators and functions provided by the language. Since these differ among the various SQL dialects, so do the encoding schemes.

For example, Figure 2 shows a system of native characteristic function encodings for numeric arguments suitable for generic Transact SQL (Sybase SQL Server 4.x; Sybase System 10; Microsoft SQL Server 4.2) [3]. A simplified version of this scheme for non-NULL arguments is also described in [8].

Encodings for basic binary comparators:

$$\delta[A=B] \qquad = 1-abs(sign(A-B))$$
$$\delta[A!=B] \qquad = abs(sign(A-B))$$
$$\delta[A<B] \qquad = 1-sign(1+sign(A-B))$$
$$\delta[A<=B] \qquad = sign(1-sign(A-B))$$
$$\delta[A>B] \qquad = 1-sign(1-sign(A-B))$$
$$\delta[A>=B] \qquad = sign(1+sign(A-B))$$

Encodings for IS NULL and IS NOT NULL operators:

$$\delta[A\ IS\ NULL] \qquad = isnull(0*A,1)$$
$$\delta[A\ IS\ NOT\ NULL] \qquad = 1-isnull(0*A,1)$$

Encoding for the logical operator NOT:

$$\delta[NOT\ \alpha] \qquad = 1-\delta[\alpha]$$

Encodings for the logical operators AND and OR for the two-valued (True or False) logic (usually applicable to data without NULLs):

$$\delta[\alpha\ AND\ \beta] \qquad = \delta[\alpha]*\delta[\beta]$$
$$\delta[\alpha\ OR\ \beta] \qquad = sign(\delta[\alpha]+\delta[\beta])$$

Encodings for the logical operators AND and OR for the three-valued (True, False or Maybe) logic (usually applicable to data with NULLs):

$\delta[\alpha \text{ AND } \beta]$ = isnull($\delta[\alpha]*\delta[\beta]$,0/(1–isnull($\delta[\alpha]$,1)*isnull($\delta[\beta]$,1)))

$\delta[\alpha \text{ OR } \beta]$ = isnull(sign($\delta[\alpha]+\delta[\beta]$),1/(isnull($\delta[\alpha]$,0)+isnull($\delta[\beta]$,0)))

Figure 2: *A system of generic Transact SQL characteristic function encodings for numeric arguments and logical operators.*

A trace of these encodings, discussed in detail in [3], shows their correctness. (Here, symbols **A** and **B** stand for numeric expressions. Symbols α and β represent logical conditions. The built-in function **sign()** returns -1, 0 and +1 for negative, zero and positive integer arguments, respectively; the built-in function **abs()** returns the absolute value of its argument. Both of these functions return floating point results for floating point arguments, and return NULL for the NULL arguments, respectively. The built-in function **isnull()** returns the first argument if it is not NULL, and returns the second argument otherwise.)

In [3], Rozenshtein, Abramovich and Birger also discuss native generic Transact SQL characteristic function encodings for arguments of other data types, including strings and datetime quantities.

We can now use the first encoding (for $\delta[A=B]$) from Figure 2 to substitute for the δ-notations in Figure 1, resulting in the syntactically correct, generic Transact SQL query shown in Figure 3.

```
SELECT name,
  janAmount = SUM(amount*(1–abs(sign(month–1)))),
  febAmount = SUM(amount*(1–abs(sign(month–2)))),
     ...
  decAmount = SUM(amount*(1–abs(sign(month–12))))
FROM bonus
GROUP BY name
```

Figure 3: *A generic Transact SQL solution for the table pivoting problem.*

4 Encoding characteristic functions in SQL-92

SQL-92 supports a row-wise CASE expression constructor, which can be used to directly define characteristic function encodings, as shown in Figure 4.

$$
\begin{aligned}
\delta[\alpha] = \text{CASE} \\
&\text{WHEN } \alpha \text{ THEN 1} &&\text{/* if } \alpha \text{ is True, return 1 */} \\
&\text{WHEN NOT } \alpha \text{ THEN 0} &&\text{/* if } \alpha \text{ is False, return 0 */} \\
&\text{ELSE NULL} &&\text{/* if } \alpha \text{ is Maybe, return NULL */} \\
\text{END}
\end{aligned}
$$

Figure 4: *Characteristic function encoding using the CASE expression constructor.*

Here symbol α stands for any syntactically valid SQL condition, whose arguments can be of any data type and which can involve logical operators NOT, AND and OR. This encoding also properly handles cases where condition α evaluates to Maybe (which may happen in the case of some arguments to α being NULL). Thus, this single encoding scheme replaces all of the cases of Figure 2.

Furthermore, because the absence of the ELSE clause in the CASE expressions is equivalent to ELSE NULL, the ELSE clause can be omitted in this case, resulting in the following simpler, but equivalent, encoding.

$$\delta[\alpha] = \text{CASE WHEN } \alpha \text{ THEN 1 WHEN NOT } \alpha \text{ THEN 0 END}$$

Note that both the encoding of Figure 4 and its simplified form above require that condition α be explicitly listed twice. If, however, α can be guaranteed to evaluate to True or False only (and not to Maybe), then the encoding can be simplified as follows (thus, listing condition α only once).

$$\delta[\alpha] = \text{CASE WHEN } \alpha \text{ THEN 1 ELSE 0 END}$$

Further simplifications are possible for various other restricted forms of condition α. For example, if α involves just a single binary comparison, e.g., **(A>B)**, and **A** and **B** are *numeric expressions*, then the following encoding will also correctly handle possible NULL **A** and/or **B** values.

δ[A>B] = CASE WHEN (A>B) THEN 1 ELSE 0*A*B END

Similarly, for other binary comparators.

If α involves just a single equality comparison (**A=B**) and does not involve NULLs, then a simpler form of the CASE expression constructor can be used.

δ[A=B] = CASE A WHEN B THEN 1 ELSE 0 END

This simplest form is sufficient for our example query, which can now be rewritten as shown in Figure 5.

An implementation directly based on the query of Figure 1:

```
SELECT name,
janAmount = SUM(amount*CASE month WHEN 1 THEN 1 ELSE 0 END),
febAmount = SUM(amount*CASE month WHEN 2 THEN 1 ELSE 0 END),
   ...
decAmount = SUM(amount*CASE month WHEN 12 THEN 1 ELSE 0 END)
FROM bonus
GROUP BY name
```

An equivalent implementation bringing **amount** *inside the THEN clauses:*

```
SELECT name,
   janAmount = SUM(CASE month WHEN 1 THEN amount ELSE 0 END),
   febAmount = SUM(CASE month WHEN 2 THEN amount ELSE 0 END),
     ...
   decAmount = SUM(CASE month WHEN 12 THEN amount ELSE 0 END)
FROM bonus
GROUP BY name
```

Figure 5: *The CASE-based implementations of the table pivoting query.*

Naturally, this solution can be used only in those systems that support the CASE expressions (e.g., Microsoft SQL Server 6.0; Red Brick Warehouse 3.5).

5 Converting zeros to NULLs

Some of the techniques presented in [1–8] rely on the ability to "convert" zeros to NULLs. In SQL-92 this can be accomplished using the CASE expressions constructor, as shown in two alternative formulations below.

CASE A WHEN 0 THEN NULL ELSE A END

CASE WHEN A!=0 THEN A END

Given some numeric expression **A**, both of these CASE expressions return NULL if **A=0** and return **A** otherwise. (Recall that omitting the ELSE clause in the second CASE expression is equivalent to ELSE NULL.)

In generic Transact SQL prior to Sybase System 10, such conversions could be accomplished using the Transact SQL property that division by 0 returns NULL, as follows.

A/sign(abs(A))

In Sybase System 10, however, the default treatment of division by 0 was changed to generate an error that aborts the computation. One way to overcome this is to force the old division by 0 behavior by starting the server with the trace flag 3610. Another is to find an alternative scheme for converting zeros to NULLs.

One such scheme, described by Snipper [9], is as follows.

A*(1–ascii(char(convert(int,abs(sign(A)))–1)))

A trace of this expression shows that it returns NULL if **A=0** and returns **A** otherwise. (Here, **A** stands for some numeric expression. The built-in function **convert(int, ...)** converts its argument to an integer. The built-in function **char()**

returns the character corresponding to the ASCII value of its operand. The built-in function **ascii()** returns the ASCII code corresponding to its character operand. All of these functions return NULL for the NULL arguments. Note that the use of **convert()** is necessary because the **char()** function requires an integer argument.)

Note that this solution relies on the fact that **char(−1)** returns NULL — a reasonable behavior since no legitimate character with the ASCII value of −1 exists. This suggests that there should be other, similar solutions, based on other built-in functions returning NULL for illegal argument values.

The first solution that comes to mind is

$$A*(1-\text{sqrt}(\text{abs}(\text{sign}(A))-1))$$

based on the expectation that the square root function **sqrt(−1)** should return NULL. Other solutions could be based on the expectation that the logarithm function **log(0)**, trigonometric cotangent function **cot(0)**, etc., should also all return NULL.

However, these solutions do not work in Sybase System 10. Without the trace flag 3610, functions **sqrt(−1)**, **log(0)**, **cot(0)**, etc., generate abort errors. With the flag, these functions return some unpredictable non-NULL floating point value. We consider the latter to be a bug, particularly since these functions used to return NULL in Sybase SQL Server 4.x, and have reported it to Sybase.

6 Alternative strategies for implementing conditional expressions in SQL

Many of the techniques of [1–8] use *row-level conditional expressions*. In SQL-92, such expressions can be implemented directly using the CASE expression constructor, as in

CASE WHEN α THEN A ELSE B END

where α represents some condition and **A** and **B** stand for some expressions.

In generic Transact SQL, if division by 0 returns NULL, then conditional expressions can be implemented as follows [2].

isnull(A/$\delta[\alpha]$, B/(1-$\delta[\alpha]$))

Here, we assume numeric and possibly NULL **A** and **B**, and a non-NULL $\delta[\alpha]$, i.e., where condition α evaluates to True or False only (and not to Maybe). A trace of this expression shows its correctness. (This trace is discussed in detail in [2], which also considers the case of NULL $\delta[\alpha]$, as well as non-numeric **A** and **B**.)

If division by 0 results in an abort error, then conditional expressions can be implemented as follows. (Here, the use of **convert()** is still necessary, since the results of the δ-expressions may be floating point — i.e., 1.0 and 0.0.)

isnull(A*(1–ascii(char(convert(int,$\delta[\alpha]$)–1)))),
              B*ascii(char(1–2*convert(int,$\delta[\alpha]$)))))

A trace of this expression shows its correctness. Specifically, if α is True, then $\delta[\alpha]=1$, and the **isnull()** expression becomes

isnull(A*1, B*NULL)

If **A** is not NULL, then this **isnull()** expression correctly returns its first argument **A**. If **A** is NULL, then this **isnull()** expression returns its second argument, which in this case is also NULL.

If α is False, then $\delta[\alpha]=0$, and the **isnull()** expression becomes

isnull(A*NULL, B*1)

which correctly returns **B**.

7 Conclusion

No matter what the DBMS, fewer passes through the data means faster SQL queries. In [1–8], Rozenshtein, Abramovich and Birger developed an SQL programming methodology, for minimizing the number of the required data passes in queries. For many types of important practical problems this methodology results in SQL solutions that are substantially more efficient than their conventional counterparts.

This methodology relies on the notion of *characteristic functions*, which are devices for encoding logical conditions as scalar expressions, returning 1 if the condition evaluates to True, returning 0 if the condition evaluates to False, and returning NULL if the condition evaluates to Maybe.

Prior to SQL-92, every SQL dialect required its own system of characteristic function encodings. Because they relied on the particular scalar operators and functions provided by the dialect, these encodings varied greatly among the different systems, and among the different data types within the same system.

With SQL-92, however, it has now become possible to use its CASE expression constructor to develop a single, and universally applicable to all data types, characteristic function encoding scheme. In this article, we show how this can be accomplished.

The existence of such a universal encoding scheme makes the task of writing SQL queries that use characteristic functions much easier. It also makes the resulting solutions system-independent and portable across all SQL-92 conformant DBMSs.

References

[1] D. Rozenshtein, A. Abramovich, E. Birger. "Single Statement SQL Solutions to the Table Pivoting and Folding Problems." In *SQL Forum Journal*, 1(12), November-December 1992.

[2] D. Rozenshtein, A. Abramovich, E. Birger. "Effective Implementation of Conditions as Expressions in SQL Queries." In *SQL Forum Journal*, 2(1), January-February 1993.

[3] D. Rozenshtein, A. Abramovich, E. Birger. "Encoding and Use of Characteristic Functions in SQL." In *SQL Forum Journal*, 2(2), March-April 1993.

[4] D. Rozenshtein, A. Abramovich, Y. Alexandrova, E. Birger. "The Power of Self-Joins: SQL Solutions to the Median and Other Row Positioning Problems." In *SQL Forum Journal*, 2(4), July-August 1993.

[5] D. Rozenshtein, A. Abramovich, E. Birger. "A Novel Approach to Computing Extreme Values in Transact SQL." In *SQL Forum Journal*, 2(5), September-October 1993.

[6] D. Rozenshtein, A. Abramovich, E. Birger. "Loop-Free SQL Solutions for Finding Continuous Regions in Data." In *SQL Forum Journal*, 2(6)-3(1), November-December 1993/January-February 1994.

[7] D. Rozenshtein, A. Abramovich, E. Birger. "SQL Solutions to Computing the Median in the Presence of Duplicates." In *SQL Forum Journal*, 3(2), March-April 1994.

[8] D. Rozenshtein, A. Abramovich, E. Birger. "Speeding Up SQL Queries — Characteristically." In *Database Programming and Design*, 8(10), October 1995.

[9] R. Snipper. Letter to the Editor. In *SQL Forum Journal*, 4(3), 1995.